RUN
YOUR
RACE

RUN
YOUR
RACE

A Guide to Making Your
Impossibles Possible

DR. MAYRA LLADÓ

Run Your Race: A Guide to Making Your Impossibles Possible

Editor: Tracy Ann Teel of Finesse Writing and Editing LLC
Cover Photo: Daniel Romero Photography
Cover and interior design: Adina Cucicov, Flamingo Designs

ISBN: 978-0-9911415-4-8

Praise for "Run Your Race"

"Brilliant! Dr. Mayra Lladó presents a powerful yet simple road map to your success. Through her inspirational stories and guides, she creates actions steps that are easy to implement. *Run Your Race* is a must read for anyone wanting to turn the impossible to possible! Get in the game and get started by reading this amazing book. Everything is possible!"

Starr Pilmore, Author, Speaker, Coach,
Creator of Fun With Visualization Program.
www.FunWithVisualization.com

"On your mark, get set, go! *Run Your Race* sets the perfect pace for getting something done—accomplishing any goal. Finding the path is, of course, the first step, as the author states, and then demonstrates through her own personal story of deciding to run her first marathon.

This is a wonderful book using the example of the challenge of a marathon to explain the actions it takes to do something you want to do. Every technique anyone would need is incorporated here—from visualization to materialization. All of this is offered up in an easy-going, non-preachy manner with inspiring stories of other people's experiences. This is a really great book for anyone trying to get off the mark and get on with it. I highly recommend it!"

Sally Huss, #1 Amazon Best-Selling Author of
"Your Survival Guide—14 Ways to Stay Afloat!"

"Mayra Llado's *Run Your Race* is a masterpiece that empowers me to get moving. She reminds me to celebrate my successes and shares specific strategies to create new ones. This is more than just a book to me. This is a gift that has truly re-ignited my fire to get back in my own race AND take things to a whole new level! This is a MUST-READ for anyone who desires to achieve high results in their life and business!"

Romeo Marquez Jr., International Motivational Speaker

www.RomeoMarquezJr.com

"This book will inspire and empower you to go for anything you previously thought was not possible in your life. Dr. Mayra has brilliantly put together a simple and easy-to-follow map for anyone anywhere to take on their biggest goals and achieve their biggest dreams. Don't sit on the sidelines watching life go by; get on the track and *Run Your Race!*"

Sean Smith, Certified Master Results Coach

www.CoachSeanSmith.com

"What an inspiring and powerful book to guide anyone to achieving their most coveted goals and desires. It is chock-full of easy to follow guidelines and step by step exercises to get you into action and to achieve what could seem impossible to start. I can vouch for these guidelines myself as I have used them to achieve personal and professional goals I couldn't have dreamed of accomplishing earlier in my life. They work! If you want to be inspired to move forward, read this book!"

Jani Ashmore, Author, Speaker, Consultant

www.janiashmore.com

"Dr Mayra Lladó's book *Run Your Race* is an uplifting collection of heart- warming stories of those who have been faced with adversities, hardships, and challenges, but pulled out all the stops to succeed! Dr. Mayra Lladó's writing style is powerful, and she has the innate ability to bring readers into each and every story as if they are bystanders watching it unfold. She has seamlessly interwoven time-tested principles and lays out a step-by-step action plan for you to be successful at every level in life or business. This book is inspiring and focused on helping any reader become a winner!"

Kellie Alderton, Healthy Living Expert, Author of
Snap Out of It: From Stress to Success Living With MS,
www.msfreeforall.com

"As I read Dr. Mayra Lladó's , *Run Your Race,* I could hear all the lessons that I learned from her in person, either by watching her daily actions or through her wonderful friendship and words of advice. Mayra's vision in this book is a way of life for her. It was through her vision and friendship that I made MY impossible possible, healing myself of a thyroid autoimmune disease, Hashimoto's.

Through the brilliant example of a marathon, which many people feel would be impossible to them, Mayra lays the ground work for accomplishing ANYTHING you might want to achieve in life, but especially those things we feel are so BIG, that they seem impossible. Have you been dreaming of an impossible that you'd like to make a possible? Walk through the simple steps that Mayra outlines, navigate your fears and obstacles, and get it done!"

Kelly Robbins, Life Coach @ Guiding Light Success Systems, Inc.
Creator of the Hashimoto's: Harbors of Healing Program
www.hashimotosharborsofhealing.com

"Mayra Lladó's *Run Your Race* is more about the journey than the "race." Anyone can set an outrageous goal—the power in making it possible lies in the persistent discovery of knowing what you need to do, who you need to become, and why you are driven to achieve it. Filled with heartfelt, inspiring stories, this book fuels possibility and unveils the timeless strategies to energize your dreams into reality!"

Nathalie Osborn, Founder www.FunEnergyNow.com

"One of the things I love about Dr. Mayra's *Run Your Race*, is that she is authentically living her words every day and truly has the life that she desires. *Run Your Race* is a compelling journey to inspire you to run your own race. What can you do to reach the finish line of life? She teaches you how to set goals, set your pace and enjoy the scenery along the way. Lastly, she is a pillar of encouragement to help you run on your pathway to success. I highly recommend following the advice and true mastery that Dr. Mayra shares from her personal experience from running her own race in life. She is truly a success!"

Amy Cady-author Get The Skinny On Your Success

www.amycady.com

"As I read Dr. Mayra Lladó's latest book, *Run Your Race*, my heart opened up to the beauty and truths she speaks in it. She moves us by the clarity and power of these success principles which she brings to life in her personal stories for all of us to learn from. A well-written treasure map for all of us who feel the tug of something we have yet to accomplish in our lives. Mayra's love for life comes through and is just as infectious in the written word as she is in person. I highly recommend owning this book, and putting what she says into practice. Here's to all your races yet to be run and the finish lines yet to be crossed!"

Samuel Johnson

www.healthierfathersbetterdads.com

"Dr. Mayra Lladó weaves a beautiful story of her own personal journey of running a marathon with proven success principles that can be used to succeed with any breakthrough life goal. In her book *Run Your Race*, Dr. Lladó inspires the reader to Go for the Goal! She'll guide you to courageously choose your personal breakthrough goal and make a plan to attain it. Once you have the clarity of where you want to go, just follow the steps in this book! Dr. Lladó convinces us that it doesn't have to be hard to live the life of our dreams. It can be as easy as putting one foot in front of the other, and before long, you will be running full speed toward the finish line and the attainment of your goal! There is no better time than right now! Buy this book and get started living the life you were meant to live!"

Tresa Leftenant ,CFP®

www.myfinancialdesign.com

"How appropriate that Dr. Mayra helps people recover their smiles. She certainly made me smile with this book. Dr. Mayra shares her own story of courage in achieving her goals in a way that gently encourages others to do the same. Her kindness comes through in her writing, and I can feel her cheering me on. She presents simple, easy to follow steps and throws in plenty of fun along the way."

Melanie Smithson, MA, LPC, BC-DMT, CHT

www.melaniesmithson.com

Author of *Stress Free in 30 Seconds*

"Take Action and do what makes you feel good. This is what Mayra's book walks, or should I say "runs" you through. I was taken back to the time that I ran a marathon and the actions that I had to create in order to accomplish my goal. *Run Your Race* will make you feel inspired and unafraid of what lays ahead."

Pete Winiarski #1 Best Selling Author

www.DailyActionLog.com

"Dr. Mayra writes with beauty and clarity about the basic human questions that vex us all—What do I want and how am I going to get it? She directly and clearly shows through personal examples and stories, evidence that the *Success Principles* as written by Jack Canfield work in our lives. Get into action and buy this book, then follow the clear directions and create the life of your dreams!"

Tom Prah Rph CPC SRC Stepping Stones to Peace LLC

www.head2heartcoach.com

"Life happens! Hours quickly turn to days, days to weeks, weeks to months, and months to years. My friend and accountability partner, Mayra Lladó, brilliantly compares life to running a marathon in *Run Your Race*. As an accomplished cosmetic dentist, business woman, success coach, loving wife, and marathon runner, Mayra knows what it takes to set her sights on a variety of big goals and to create incremental steps for achieving them in record time resulting in an incredible life many only dream of experiencing. This fast-paced book will inspire and teach you how to become your best self and create the life of your dreams—stride by stride!"

Denny Noneman—Commercial Real Estate Broker—Toledo, Ohio

"The book *Run Your Race* is one of my grand favorites for two reasons. First, it came into my life at the right moment, just when I was ready to take full advantage of it's lessons. Second: it's content. Mayra presents us with universal foundations to grow and reach success in our lives. She explains them in simple terms, clearly and direct. That is what is so special about this book. The analogy of running a race, going step by step towards our goals…enjoying the journey, even when it gets difficult. Thank you Mayra!"

Cristóbal Colón

www.cristobalcolon.net

"If you are looking for how to overcome obstacles that stop you from achieving your goals and reaching success, this book is for you. With stories and anecdotes based on her experience of overcoming challenges towards her goal of running her first marathon, in *Run Your Race*, Dr. Mayra Llado, presents simple strategies of personal growth that will allow you to discover how to align your life, relationships and dreams to overcome any obstacle with success. Just run your race, Mayra will take you by the hand with this inspiring story.

Martiña Reyes. NLP Master Mentor
www.TheMindPowerLab.com

"This book has soul, the author Mayra Lladó is a brilliant woman and excellent communicator of values. This is how she approaches life, and this book you have in your hands is the result of a lot of time and dedication in order to teach by example. In a simple and practical manner it proposes how to achieve your objectives to help you believe in the impossible. It's at the top!

Lourdes Carmona
www.listosparadespegue.com

"Dr. Mayra Llado in her book; *Run Your Race* shares easy to implement action steps and time-tested success principles that have helped her and many others turn what seemed impossible into possible and achieve their dreams. It's a quick, fun and heartwarming read yet very powerful in its message. Apply the action steps at the end of each chapter and you will experience tremendous growth and take your life to the next level of success and fulfillment."

Carlos y Cecy Marin, International Trainer, Speaker
and Author of the best seller *The Ultimate Success Formula*
www.carlosmarin.com

Motivate and Inspire Others!

"Share this book"

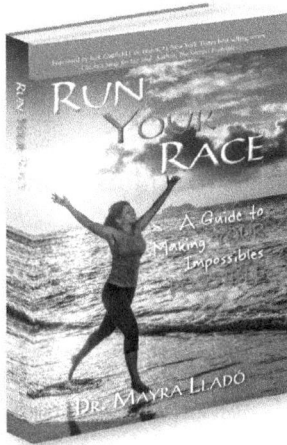

Retail $18.88

Special Quantity Discounts

5-20 Books	$16.88
21-99 Books	$14.88
100-499 Books	$12.88
500-999 Books	$10.88
1,000+ Books	$8.88

To Place an Order Contact:

info@mayrallado.com

www.mayrallado.com

www.runyourracebook.com

THE IDEAL PROFESSIONAL SPEAKER FOR YOUR NEXT EVENT!

Any organization that wants to develop their people to become "extraordinary", needs to hire Dr. Mayra Lladó for a keynote and/or workshop training.

To contact or book Dr. Mayra Lladó to speak at your next event:

info@mayrallado.com
www.mayrallado.com
FaceBook: Dr. Mayra Llado
Instagram: drmayra8

Download Your *Run Your Race* **Training Guide—Free!**—To accompany and implement the strategies you will find in this book.

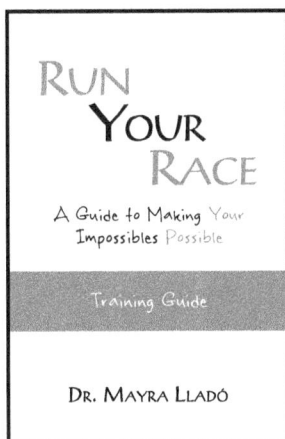

RUN
YOUR
RACE

A Guide to Making Your
Impossibles Possible

Training Guide

DR. MAYRA LLADÓ

Get it at www.runyourracebook.com

This book is dedicated to my soul mate and life partner, my husband Antonio, and to all of you who want to be more, do more, and have more in your life.

Table of Contents

Foreword

Many people don't live the life they truly desire because they put limits on what they think they can or cannot do. Part of my life's mission and purpose has been to inspire and empower people to live their highest vision.

Dr. Mayra Lladó is one of those people. She has been intensely involved in discovering and living her life's purpose, by applying these principles of success and by tapping into her passions and potential.

I have personally witnessed her journey of transformation over the years as my student in many of my training programs. She walks the talk. Both she and her husband have served as training assistants in my Breakthrough to Success program as well as my Train the Trainer program. Mayra walks the talk. And now she runs the race.

I am honored and proud to support her in this work of love and inspiration. In *Run Your Race*, she shares the principles she has used and steps she has taken to accomplish goals that seemed impossible to her, at first. Making the impossible possible is her crowning achievement.

Her gift of simplifying a concept and creating an effortless way to communicate that to the reader makes for an enjoyable and inspirational book.

Whether you are a runner, walker or couch potato, the stories and action steps in this book will help you discover what things you truly want to be, do or have while providing concrete action steps to turn your impossibles into possibles.

Jack Canfield
Co-creator, #1 New York Times Best selling series *Chicken Soup for the Soul*, Author, *The Success Principles*
www.jackcanfield.com

Acknowledgements

This book was inspired by a picture book I created after running my first marathon October 21st of 2006. Many people read it and enjoyed the pictures and encouraged me to write about how I went about accomplishing such a big goal to inspire others in their lives to do the same.

I want to thank these people as well as all the others who have contributed to the birth of this labor of love.

First and foremost, I want to thank my mother Leticia for her example of determination and persistence. She is my hero and has inspired me to always go for my dreams. I want to also thank my father Victor for being a great example to me of diversifying oneself and having the courage to do things differently.

I am forever grateful for my husband Antonio and his unconditional love and support in everything I do. You are my love, my best friend, my partner, my mentor, my husband; you enhance everything about me.

My family and close friends—for being my rocks and always encouraging me with my projects and goals. Especially my sisters Monica and Rosana, my friends Nelissa and Gustavo, Vilma, Ernesto, Carly and Tito.

I want to acknowledge my mentor Jack Canfield for dedicating his life to helping others discover their true potential and live out their highest vision. You have truly inspired me with your authenticity, generosity, and living example that these principles work when we work them.

Patty Aubrey—for being such a great role model for me in what it means to go after your dreams and believe it is possible.

Jack Canfield Training Group—you are all rock stars! Thank you for always being so encouraging and supportive of all I do. Jesse, Andrea, Jody, Donna, Lisa, Veronica.

My friend Kellie—for always being one of my rocks, for having the faith and confidence in me to get on an airplane and fly to Lake Arrowhead to write her book, and for encouraging and supporting me in writing mine.

Jan Fraser—for being an inspiration and an incredible mentor and coach during this writing journey; you are like a mom to me.

My accountability partners Ricky, Nathalie and Denny. Without your support, encouragement, and above all, your efforts to keep me accountable, I am sure this book would have taken much longer to get into print.

Members of my Master Mind Groups: Michelle, Cindy, Ameesha, Nita, Monique, Rebecca, Saima, Samuel, Tom and Kelly. You have all been through most of this journey alongside me. Your feedback and support has been invaluable.

Jackie and Alex—you both have served as inspiration for great accountability as well as encouragement to me. I am forever grateful to you both.

Sean—thanks for being my coach, my sounding board, and such a great listener. You may not be aware of how much you have helped me throughout this whole process.

Michelle and Jeff—for your wonderfully inspiring story; I am sure it will touch many as it has me.

Thank you Natalie for sharing your story during our time together in Train the Trainer and for allowing me to include it in this book as I am sure it will inspire many.

Doña Ana—for being a great inspiration for all! You demonstrate the power of having a dream and going for it no matter how old or in what situation you find yourself.

Greg—for being such a great friend and inspiration. Thank you for giving me the privilege and honor of being part of your first marathon.

Chewi—for being such a great trainer, mentor, coach, and accountability partner. Thank you for sharing your heart and leadership with so many others in our beautiful Island of Puerto Rico, and beyond. You truly are a man of character and service.

I would also like to acknowledge and thank Rick and Dick Hoyt for being such inspirations to me and the thousands and thousands of others whose lives they have touched.

I would like to thank: Charlie Engle, Ray Zehab, and Kevin Lin. What you set out to accomplish is something the majority of people would never even consider attempting; you are a true example of what it takes to make the impossible possible. You have inspired me beyond words. I also want to acknowledge Matt Damon for the production of the documentary, *Running the Sahara*, and also for co-founding www.H2OAfrica.org along with the runners. Now, together with water partners, what is now www.water.org, you're helping put clean, safe water in everyone's hands.

Last, but not least, I would like to acknowledge all the people who have had the courage and determination to go for their dreams in spite of all perceived obstacles and limitations; you inspire me and make me proud. Thank you for running your race!

Introduction

Most of the time when I tell people I've run a marathon, they seem amazed and say "WOW! I could never do that." That's exactly what I thought before I decided that I wanted to run my first marathon. I had run in high school, and after running one day on the street I got really bad shin splints. I decided that running wasn't for me.

In 2004 while looking in the mirror, I said to the person looking back at me, "Who are you? Whose life are you living?" Bang! Right between the eyes! It definitely was not MY LIFE; I felt like I was living someone else's life. Wow! Now what? I wasn't sure how I was going to do it; I just knew that I had to stop living someone else's life and start living my own!

That was the day that I was done settling. It was the day that I not only began designing the life that I wanted, but it was also the beginning of living the life that I had dreamed about. That decision unleashed a number of key events which have led me to where I find myself today.

The first step was reclaiming my life! Running provided the outlet which allowed me to slowly start to regain and match what was happening inside of me with what was happening outside of me. A friend of mine suggested that I start running. To be honest, I thought he was completely nuts! I thought, "Running? Oh my God, that is so boring!" "Not so," he said, "come run the trail in Central Park with us sometime."

One day I showed up and we ran about four miles. I thought "that wasn't so bad. It was actually kind of fun and energizing." I was pleasantly surprised by how great I felt after running. From this singular experience, I was hooked.

The following day was... not so fun... since my legs were really sore from the run, and I had gotten some blisters from not having the right shoes. That day I went to a running apparel store and bought myself a pair of running shoes, then I got myself a number of running outfits. All color coordinated, of course! I even bought myself a watch to keep track of my pace and lap times. If you didn't know me, you'd think I was an elite runner!

I began running a couple days a week, then three, then four, then I started doing long weekend runs beginning at 4:30 am! YES, I KNOW IT'S VERY EARLY! Here in Puerto Rico it can get really warm, so if you plan on running more than six miles, it's a good idea to start early when the temperature is cooler.

It wasn't long before I decided to run a 10K (6.2 mile race). For me, this was huge! I continued to run farther and did many 10K races and a few half marathons.

In 2006, two years after my first four mile run, I decided that I wanted to run a full marathon. 26.2 miles! I really didn't know how I was supposed to do it; all I knew was that others had done it before me, and now I wanted to do it as well. There's one thing to remember though: you don't just decide to run a marathon and go out and run one. Marathon running is just like any other goal, big or small. Climbing a mountain, completing an Iron Man event, starting your own business, or learning a new language. Whatever your goal is, there are principles you apply and follow in order to succeed.

After running my first marathon, I literally felt as if I could do anything! I never thought I would ever do that. Because I did, it has given me the courage and confidence to do anything I set my mind to, even if I don't initially know how or where to begin. All I have to do is apply the principles to whatever my next big goal is, take action one step at a time, and eventually I get there.

If you have always wanted to do something really big and didn't know how, this book is for you. If you have been afraid of taking risks and getting outside your comfort zone in order to achieve the things you want, this book is for you. If you have been waiting for the perfect moment to do the things that are really important to you, the things that will stretch you, then this book is for you. For the you who wants to be unstoppable, the you who wants to breakthrough to another level in your life.

You will learn in this book how to do what you love and achieve your dreams on your terms.

Chapter 1

The Question That Can Change Your Life

" *Your time is limited, so don't waste it living someone else's life. Don't be trapped by dogma—which is living with the results of other people's thinking. Don't let the noise of others' opinions drown out your own inner voice. And most important, have the courage to follow your heart and intuition. They somehow already know what you truly want to become. Everything else is secondary."*

Steve Jobs

What would you do if you knew you couldn't fail? Would you climb a mountain? Lose weight? Complete an Iron Man event? Run a marathon? Start your own business? Write a book? Live in another country? Reveal your love for someone? Skydive?

In 2006, I decided to run my first marathon. A marathon is a 26.2 mile race. I had been running for a couple of years and had done some 10K runs, but that was the extent of my running. Up to that point, 13 miles was the longest run I had completed. Making a 26.2 mile decision was scary but exciting at the same time. Even though I didn't know how I was going to manage it, I knew that when I did do it I would feel like I could accomplish anything.

Answer The Question

So what would you do if you knew you could not fail? Remember, the only way you can fail at anything is to quit or to never get started. When you answer this question it allows you to unearth your true desires and dreams, to really tap into your passions. The majority of people that don't have what they want, or are not living with passion, simply haven't decided what it is that they truly want.

> In a child's mind, there are no limits.

Have you noticed how kids have no trouble with this one? They know what they want, they voice it and persist until they get it. Another thing that children do is think with incredible imagination. In a child's mind, there are no limits. A patient of mine brought his 5-year-old daughter, Sofia, in for a dental cleaning. I began to tell him that Sofia reminded me of my niece Irene who is also the same age. I shared Irene's wishes of going to England to meet the boys in the singing group "One Direction." My patient said "What a coincidence. Ask Sofia what she wants to do in England." So I asked. "Sofia, tell me what you want to do in England." Sofia quickly replied, "I am going to build a hotel, and it is going to have three pools and, you know, one of those places where you can have somebody give you a massage." I said, "A spa?"

"Yes, a spa!" she replied, "And you can bring your dog because dogs can stay with you at the hotel. Oh... and it's going to be free." Talk about having clarity! I could literally see her hotel as she was describing it to me with such enthusiasm and confidence.

So what happened to that child in you? Can you still dream that big? Many people have buried their ability to dream along with their confidence in becoming, doing, or having the things they most desire in their heart. Often, this is a result of programming that comes from our parents, teachers, coaches, peers, and even the media. Things which you may have heard as a child or even as an adult. These may have included:

- "Don't touch that."
- "Stay away from there."
- "Money doesn't grow on trees, you know."
- "You don't want to do that."
- "Why would you want to do something like that?"
- "You don't really feel that way."
- "You will never be successful at that."

I could literally fill up the rest of this book with programming phrases. Were there phrases which you heard a lot while growing up? Can you see how they may be limiting your vision for yourself and your life?

In order to live out your passions, you need to rediscover your inner child. You can reconnect with your inner child and take your power back. There are several techniques and strategies to help you do just that very thing.

Reclaim Your Power

My husband and I were teaching this concept to our daughter, Claudia Sofia, when she was turning 14. We asked "Claudia, what do you want to do for your birthday?" She said, "I don't know." Sound familiar? So I followed up with another question. "Claudia, if you did know, what would you want to do?"

Have you ever responded with the following when asked for your input on something?

- "I don't know"
- "Whatever you want"
- "I don't care"
- "It doesn't matter to me"
- "Whatever"

> The truth is that even though we think we did not make a choice, we did... we chose not to choose.

In all of those instances, you actually gave the power of choice away to another person. Why? Most of the time we want to please the other person; other times, it is more comfortable for someone else to decide because if it doesn't turn out great, then we can say we had nothing to do with it. Or did we? The truth is that even though we think we did not make a choice, we did...we chose not to choose.

So the next time someone asks you what you would like to eat or what you'd like for your birthday, instead of saying, "I don't know." or "It doesn't matter," ask yourself "If I did know, what would I eat?" or "If it did matter, what would I want." You've got this! By making small choices like this, you will begin the process of taking your power back and unearthing the inner child who was once alive and kicking in you with great dreams and desires. The child who knew no limits.

The 5-Minute "What Do You Want" Challenge

To take this to the next level and really begin to understand what it is that you want in your heart of hearts, take the time to discover it. "How?" you might be thinking. It's quite complex actually. Begin with a friend or loved one whom you really respect and trust, and have that person ask you, "What do you want?" over and over again for five minutes. You can do this with your eyes closed if you prefer; it may allow you to concentrate deeper because you won't be worrying about how the other person is responding to your answers since you won't be looking at her or him. Have your companion write down every single thing you say. This exercise can be very profound as in the beginning you may find yourself saying things that you want which are tangible, and end up with things, as you really get into it, which are more intangible. For example love, joy, peace, bliss, adventure, etc.

101 Goals

Another fun thing to do is to sit down and answer the question: What would you do if you knew you could not fail? Or perhaps: What would you do if money was not an issue? List 101 things that you want to be, do, or have before you leave this earth. My husband, Antonio, and I did this before we were married. We went out to dinner one night, and I had brought some lined cardstock and colored pens with me. I handed him a few sheets and a pen and said to him, "Okay. We are going to create our 101 goals list."

He looked at me like "what?" and I said, "Trust me. This is going to be fun. Just write down anything that you want to be, do or have before leaving this earth. And there are no limits! Money is not an issue, and the only way you could fail is by not going after it at all or by quitting."

So we each wrote on our cardstock, and after 15 minutes we checked in with each other. It was so exciting! As we shared what we had written, we noticed we had a number of items that were the same; also, I started to get ideas from the things Antonio had on his list and vice versa. We continued for another 15 minutes and shared again. We had so much fun that evening dreaming together!

We have accomplished many of the things we wrote down that night. We've been to Disney twice with our whole family; we have seen Andrea Bocelli, Yanni, and Journey in concert. We've gone wine tasting in California in a convertible, been to Las Vegas for fun, and have run marathons in two different countries: Buenos Aires, Argentina and Berlin, Germany. Been married on the beach, started a business together, shared the same stage, and made many new friends that enhance our life. We live in a state of gratitude, look for opportunities in challenges, and the list goes on and on and on....

So how would you rate the quality of your life so far on a scale of 1 to 10 (with 1 being not too great, nothing to write home about, totally unremarkable, and 10 being completely fulfilled, joyful, excited, full of love, both given and received. Essentially, living in the full expression of your life's purpose.) Whatever the number, ask yourself: "Why so high?" Write down everything which makes this rating true. Next, ask yourself: "What would it take to make it a 10?" This is where you can take your life to the next level. Give it real thought. If you have already done some of the things I have mentioned in this chapter, then you have an idea of how you can make it happen.

Take 100% Responsibility

Many people go through life thinking that they are somehow unlucky or victims of some sort because things just never go their way. These are the people who are not taking responsibility for their lives and are just going along for the ride with those who have and are on a clear path. The good news is you always have a choice. You can decide today to take 100% responsibility for our lives and wellbeing. What this means is that you can control your thoughts, our behaviors, and the visual images that we focus on.

For example, have you ever noticed how two people in the same situation can be having two completely different experiences? My husband and I were taking care of our niece and nephew (ages 5 and 4) one night. My brother-in-law Che called to let me know he was coming by to pick them up. We live in a seven story building, and we are on the third floor. It's an old building, and the elevator light is sometimes on, other times off. This was one of those "off" times. While we were getting into the elevator, we were listening to some songs on my i-phone since my nephew is really into music. The door closed, and we noticed that the elevator was not moving.

This had happened to me a few weeks before. My husband, Antonio, turned on his phone flashlight, and I noticed he had brought a couple of Medallas, our local beer (one for my brother-in-law and one for himself). He proceeded to open one and handed it to me while opening the other for himself. After we clinked the cans together and said "salud," he proceeded to call our upstairs neighbor, then the elevator company, while I called my brother-in-law letting him know "we were on our way down."

Irene, Joaquin, Antonio, and I were dancing and singing in the elevator while we waited for someone to open the door. My brother-in-law called a few minutes later to see what was going on. I told him "Yes. We're on our way down. Just waiting for Papo our neighbor to help us with something. We will be right down." By this time it had been close to five minutes, so I texted my brother-in-law to let him know we were in the elevator waiting for our neighbor or the elevator tech to open the door so we could come down.

> You can create the outcome you want by changing your response.

Papo was finally able to open the door, and we made our way down the stairs. It was a great adventure for the four of us! Unfortunately, Che's Medalla never made it to him. This was great fun for us because of the way we chose to respond to the event. Our experience or outcome could have been very different if we had chosen to have a different response. If it would have been our next door neighbor who was stuck in the elevator, we may have had to call an ambulance in addition to the elevator maintenance people, in case she had a heart attack or something.

We all have the power within us to choose how we respond to the different events that we face on a daily basis. You can create the outcome you want by changing your response.

Imaginary Negative Outcomes And Fear

So what stops you from even trying to do the things you want to do? Excuses, fear, not knowing how to do the thing you want to do, lack of self-confidence, getting ready to get ready, not believing it is possible for you. So, how do you remove these obstacles and go for the prize?

What are some of the common fears you can face which can become obstacles, keeping you from enjoying the things you want?

- Fear of failure
- Fear of rejection
- Fear of being judged
- Fear of looking foolish
- Fear of losing
- Fear of not knowing what to do

You can probably think of many others. So what is fear? Many thought-leaders describe fear as being "False Experiences Appearing Real (FEAR)." We scare ourselves by imagining negative results or outcomes when we attempt to do the thing we want or need to do. To overcome this, write down how you scare yourself out of doing something. For example: let's say you want to ask your boss for a raise. How do you scare yourself out of doing it? Do you imagine the answer will be no? So what has changed? Nothing changes if the answer is no. Now, what if the answer is yes? Then, you would be making more money. Do you see how you may be missing opportunities because of fear? Always ask yourself how you are scaring yourself out of taking actions towards your goals and desires.

Sometimes it's not as simple as that, and there may be limiting beliefs at the root of your fear. As a friend of mine shared with me recently, there are only two real fears: one is the fear of falling, and the other is the fear we experience as a result of an unexpected, loud noise. The rest are learned behaviors.

There are many ways you can replace a limiting belief with an empowering one, so if you discover this may be at the root of your fears, you may want to consider using one of them. Among them are EFT (Emotional Freedom Technique, The Sedona Method, RIM Method, and NLP (neurolinguistic programming) You can find more information on these and some of the resources available to learn how to use them in the resources section of this book.

Victory Log

So how can you gain confidence and faith? One really cool way is to review your previous successes. This is sometimes referred to as a victory log. There are several ways to do this. You can divide your life into thirds and list your successes from the first third, second third, and the last third. Then to really get your juices flowing, you can list the successes you would like to have in the next third. You might be thinking right now: "But I haven't had many successes in my life. This might be depressing!" Well let's examine this: when you were a baby, did you just know how to walk or talk? Oh wait, how about this one: did you know how to ride a bike? You were not just born knowing these things; rather you learned how to do them. Other things in your successes might include learning to play an instrument or a sport, learning to cook, helping someone out, getting your driver's license, etc. I'm sure you are thinking of many others by now.

Keeping a daily log or journal of your wins and successes can help. This is something you can do right before going to bed. Besides your wins, a good thing to do either first thing in the morning or before going to bed is to also list the things that you ex-

> Focusing on the things that you have and that you are thankful for will make you more receptive to receiving and experiencing more of what you enjoy and want.

perienced during the day or that you are grateful for in general. Focusing on the things that you have and that you are thankful for will make you more receptive to receiving and experiencing more of what you enjoy and want.

Chapter 1 Action Steps

"Twenty years from now you will be more disappointed by the things you didn't do than by the ones you did do. So throw off the bowlines, sail away from the safe harbor. Catch the trade winds in your sails. Explore. Dream. Discover."

Mark Twain

1. Answer the question: What would you do if you could not fail?
2. Take your power back and exercise your right to choose when given the opportunity.
3. Ask a trusted loved one or friend to challenge you for five minutes by repeatedly asking "What do you want?" and write down all your answers.
4. Make a list of 101 goals.
5. Take 100% responsibility. You can create the outcome you want by changing your response.
6. Stop imagining negative outcomes and eliminate your fear.
7. Create a Victory log of your wins and daily successes.

Chapter 2

Where Do You Start?

❝When you know what you want, and want it bad enough, you will find a way to get it.”

Jim Rohn

When I decided to run my first marathon I really did not know which one to run, how to train for it, or even how I would be able to participate. It was a totally new world for me. The one thing that I did know was that I wanted to do it, and that I wanted to do it *that year* in 2006.

By this time, I had been running for a couple of years and had run a number of 10k races and a couple 21k races here in Puerto Rico. I had made many friends since I started running and noticed some of them were part of different running clubs. I figured it might be a good idea to join a club since they seemed to plan on running marathons together and supported each other in training. So that's what I did. I chose to join the club that my coach led.

I found people to talk to about their experiences of running a marathon. People that had done what I wanted to do and had succeeded at it. I also told my coach that I wanted to run a marathon, and I wanted him to train me for it. He asked if I knew which one I wanted to run, and I said that I didn't. I asked him, "Which one do you recommend I do?" "Our running club is going to go to the New York City Marathon this year." he said. "Why don't you try to get into that one?" So I asked how to get in. He said, "You have to sign up for the lottery or you have to qualify by time." So I registered for the lottery. Over 100,000 people register for the New York City Marathon every year and only 47,000 get to run it.

When the time came for the lottery draw, my name was not picked. I thought "now what?" I went to my coach and said, "What other marathon do you think I could run?" He said I should try Chicago. So I went online to the Chicago Marathon site to register and found that their registration had closed; they had reached their capacity of 40,000 registrants. Now what? I kept looking until I found a marathon tours site that had an entry for the Chicago Marathon. All I had to do was book my hotel through them, and they guaranteed my entry into the marathon. "YES! My persistence paid off." I had begun. I was registered for the race; I knew when it was happening, and where it was happening. Now I just needed to prepare myself to be able to run 26.2 miles on October 22, 2006 in Chicago. It was the first week of June, so I had 16 weeks to train.

Choose One Goal and Focus

So how are you doing? Do you know what you want to accomplish? You may be either extremely excited right now or extremely overwhelmed... or both. So where do you start? First, take a look at that list you made. Clarify your goal and put a time frame on it. Choose something. Choose the one thing to accomplish which will make you feel like you can do anything!

Now focus. Be extremely clear about this goal and fill in every detail. For example, if your goal is to speak a different language, then you need to choose which language you want to learn to speak.

"If you don't know where you are going, you'll wind up someplace else"

Yogi Berra

Otherwise, how will you know if you accomplished your goal? As Yogi Berra says, "If you don't know where you are going, you'll wind up someplace else." And how will you know what your next logical step is if you are not specific?

I was recently helping one of our workshop participants with this. He had written down a few goals, and I asked him to read them to me. He started with the financial goal. "I want to have more money," he said. So I handed him a dollar and said, "There. You *have* more money." He looked at me puzzled. "In order for you to get what you really want," I said, "you have to be very clear and specific about it because the universe will work to help you get it. See it already worked." "But I want to make more money than that," he said. I asked him how much more. "Well I don't know," he said. I said "If you did know, how much more would you want to make?"

This is the important part. Your goal should be measurable in space and time. How much? By when? Be specific so that you and anyone else can verify if you have done it or not. It is also a way to always be able to assess how close or far away you are from accomplishing it. It is very hard to hit a target you are not aware of or not focused on. On the other hand, when you know what your target is and you are focused on it, you can hit it much faster and with greater ease.

Find A Mentor Or Coach

Something that really motivated me when I decided to run the marathon was that it seemed to be such a big thing for me to do. I had never run that distance before, but at the same time I knew of others who had, so it made it seem possible. I didn't know how yet; I just knew it could be done. Find people that have done the thing you want to do. You can find them through books, in your community, or online. If you can find someone in your community, the advantage is that they may be willing and able to coach you on accomplishing your goal. Online can work as well with Skype and other means of online communication. Distance is not an obstacle any longer.

> Find people that have done the thing you want to do.

Research Your Goal

What is holding you back? We usually hold ourselves back. We put limits on what we think we can or cannot do. Or is it that you don't know of anyone who has done the thing that you want to do. If you have no evidence that it can be done, why should you even bother? This is where things can get very exciting.

I recently watched the documentary *Running the Sahara*. It is the story of three runners who decided that they wanted to be the first to run across the Sahara Desert. When they originally set this goal, all they knew was the what and the why. It took them two years to plan the expedition. They ran over 4,800 miles in 111 days through six countries. That they decided to be the pioneers is what makes the story amazing.

There always has to be a pioneer, someone or a group of people that decide they want to blaze the trail. Roger Bannister was a pioneer. He broke the four minute mile. After he did, many others followed. For this type of pioneer goal, you will still want to look for the most similar goal to yours that has been accomplished. This gives you a model of how to get close to your goal. It might require more of that action or different actions.

Review Your Victory Log Often

Review your Victory Log when self doubt sets in. Remember you did not know how to do many things initially, and yet you learned how to do them and now they are second nature to you. The "how" is not important at this point. The "what" and the "why" are what matters now.

Your Why

The "what" is your goal. Let's address the "why." Why is it important? The "why" drives you to continue moving forward towards your goal. When I was

The easiest way to really dig down to your "why" is by acting like a curious child.

training my sales teams in the past and we were working on goal setting, I would ask them to write down 20 reasons why they wanted to accomplish their goals. I explained that these would be instrumental to keep them motivated and to remind them when things got tough.

The easiest way to really dig down to your "why" is by acting like a curious child. You know how children will endlessly ask you "why?" You answer, then they ask "why?" again until you get to "because that's the way it is." So for example, I wanted to run a full marathon. "Why?" Because I wanted to challenge myself. "Why?" Because I wanted to accomplish something big. "Why?" Because it would give me the confidence to go after other big goals. "Why?" Because less than 1% of the U.S. population can say they have completed a marathon.

A more powerful version of the why question is: "Why is that important?" Returning to my example about the marathon, I asked myself, "Why is that important?" Because I never thought that I could do it? "Why is that important?" Because I knew that if I did do it, I could do just about anything. "Why is that important?" Because then I can be, do, or have anything if I set my mind to it.

How about you? Answer these questions:

- Why do you want to accomplish your goal?
- What does it mean to you?
- What does it mean to your family?
- What does it mean to your business?
- Who will you become in the process?
- What opportunities will it bring?
- How will it make you feel to have accomplished it?

Can you get excited about this? YES YOU CAN!

Share Your Goal

Now that you are excited, share your goal and your vision with the people you care about most. Your spouse, your children, your close friends. Even with your dog or cat if you have one. Explain to them what is involved in achieving this goal, especially what is in it for them when you do it. This will ensure they are in your corner and rooting for you right from the beginning.

Natalie's Story

I met Natalie during one of Jack Canfield's trainings where I was assisting. She lives in Los Angeles and during our training she gave a presentation in which she shared the story of when she ran her first marathon. When I asked Natalie what motivated her to want to run a marathon, she shared with me that it was something that had always been on her bucket list. Besides being on her list of 101 goals, she decided she wanted to do it for Charity knowing that would inspire her to train and be able to finish the race. She would be running in the Honolulu Marathon taking place December 9, 2001. She decided that she would raise money for Aids Project LA. She said to me "once I raised $4,000 my airfare was paid for, so I had to get on that plane and run that race!"

Natalie shared her goal with anyone who would listen. The more people she told, the more support she received, and, in turn, the more committed she became to it. Some of the people she had shared her goal with had also run a marathon and told her that it was the hardest thing they had ever done. She said "to be honest, that inspired me even more!"

A couple of months before she was to fly to Honolulu for the marathon, an airplane flew into the Twin Towers in New York City and caused them to collapse. It was a time when many people became afraid to travel on airplanes. Many people tried to talk Natalie out of following through with her goal. She was so clear on her why and so committed that it never entered her mind not to go ahead with it.

A week before the marathon, Natalie learned that her childhood friend Lizzie, who was living in San Francisco, would also be running in the race. This became yet another strong reason for Natalie to accomplish this goal; now she had the opportunity to do it with someone she knew and cared about.

As long as you are clear on the "what" and the "why," the "how" will begin to unfold once you start.

So what do you need to do? Choose your goal, get clear on it, and put a date on it. Research people who have achieved what you want to achieve. Find out if you have the knowledge and skill set needed to accomplish your goal. If not, learn about the new skills you'll need. Remember, as long as you are clear on the "what" and the "why," the "how" will begin to unfold once you start. So just start!

Chapter 2 Action Steps

"You can have anything you want, if you want it badly enough. You can be anything you want to be, do anything you set out to accomplish if you hold to that desire with singleness of purpose."

Abraham Lincoln

1. Choose one goal to focus on.
2. Be very clear on the goal and put a time frame on it. (How much, by when?)
3. Find a mentor or coach (through books, online, or in your community)
4. Do research on your goal. (What skills are needed to accomplish your goal?)
5. Review your Victory Log often.
6. Write your reasons for wanting to accomplish your goal. (Display them where you can see them daily.)
7. Share your goal with your inner circle. (spouse, children, close friends)

Chapter 3

Just Do It!

" *Faith is taking the first step even when you don't see the whole staircase."*

Martin Luther King

Once you know what you want with great clarity and detail, have put a time frame in place to achieve it, and determined your next logical step, guess what comes next? YES! You must take the next step!

What separates the successful from the unsuccessful is action. Whether your goal is to run a marathon, get your degree, have your own business, start a non-profit, or something entirely different, the next step would be to show up for training, register for the marathon, go to your government office and apply for a business license, have a meeting with the person in your community that has already started a non-profit. You get the idea.

Stop talking about what you want to do and JUST DO IT!

Stop talking about what you want to do and JUST DO IT!

At this point, many people can suffer from what I call the "getting ready to get ready syndrome". One time I had this idea for a business, and I started to put it together in my mind, and I talked about it a lot to my friends and family. I did research and research and research, and you guessed it, *more research*. The funny thing about this is that I thought I was accomplishing so much by researching and making sure that I knew every detail about this business idea before I actually took a step. This is also referred to as paralysis of analysis, where you feel you have to know absolutely every thing under the sun before you can actually start! So did I ever start that business? The answer is no because I researched myself out of business. *It was exhausting!*

Take The First Step

What I learned from this experience is that things don't have to be perfect in order for you to start and be successful. Recently, Antonio and I were preparing for one of our "Ignite Your Success" workshops. We went to Sam's Club where we usually have our workbooks printed. Jose, the fellow who was helping us, printed out a proof copy for us to approve before printing the actual workbooks. When he did, we noticed that somehow the pages had shifted and were not corresponding with the original layout. The file had been created in Word on my Mac, so when Jose opened the file in Word on his P.C. it changed all the formatting and fonts. He suggested that I change the original on my computer and email it or bring it back the next day.

We came back the next morning and Sheila, who was the manager, was the one on duty. She was very timid and did not project much confidence in what she was doing. I gave her my pen drive with the file, so she could print out another proof copy. I began to page through it and...uh-oh...page five had a kind of hieroglyphics look. Instead of text, there were a bunch of squares in the place where the letters should have been. This was occurring on pages 5 through 7. She tried to figure out why this was happening. Oh, did I mention it was 7:30 am on the day of our workshop, and that we were to be at the location at 8:30 am? Antonio is very punctual and gets stressed out when we are running against the clock. I was sitting in front of Sheila sending her positive energy and thoughts. "Sheila, you are going to solve this for me."

It was now 8:15 am and still no progress. Antonio was getting very anxious. Sheila had been able to print the weird squares pages separately, and they came out fine. All of a sudden Antonio said, "It doesn't have to be perfect; we can make it work. We will tell them what should be written in the squares, and they can write it in." I said, "Okay Sheila. Let's print out the separate pages, and we will have our participants insert them." This actually worked out perfectly because it allowed us to use the experience as a teaching point in our workshop on this very topic of taking action and not waiting until something is perfect. We did end up with our workbook, just not how we envisioned it originally. It ended up being even better because it allowed us to visually make the point with our participants.

Stop waiting for the perfect moment, for the perfect day, for the right person to show up, for the right font for your book, for inspiration, for every detail to be clear, for someone to tell you what to do. JUST TAKE THE FIRST STEP!

Divide Into Manageable Actions

When you are starting a new endeavor or taking the first step towards your big or small goal, it can feel overwhelming at first. Take your goal and divide it into manageable actions that when put together get you to your destination. There is a saying that illustrates this: "By the inch it's a cinch; by the mile it's a trial."

"By the inch it's a cinch... by the mile it's a trial."

When I started training for my first marathon, I approached it week by week and day by day, instead of focusing on details like training for 16 weeks and running 20 miles at least once before my marathon. These details would have overwhelmed me and made me doubt myself. My coach would send me my training schedule for the week; I would review it and see if I had to make any adjustments, like which day would be my rest day, in order to fit in with the rest of my obligations. I did this to make sure there was no room for missing my training.

Besides training, I considered my diet—which foods would give my body more energy, fuel, and support in order to be more effective during my training sessions. I also made sure I was hydrating myself enough by drinking water throughout the day and during my practice. I made sure that I was getting enough rest. Our bodies need rest in order to repair, regenerate, and strengthen the muscles we are working, and our system and cells need it as a whole in order to ensure we have the energy to keep going the next day.

My training was far from perfect. There were days when I did not eat that well or when I went out with friends and we had some drinks. There were even days when I was either too tired or had made something else more important than taking action towards my goal. Yes, I would feel like a loser for a little while and beat myself up for not keeping my agreements with myself. Then I would remember that the only way I could fail at this goal was if I **QUIT**. The next day I would show up for training and move myself one step further on the journey towards my goal.

> The only way you can fail is if you QUIT.

Strategy:
Divide your goal into manageable daily actions.

Reminder:
The only way you can fail is if you QUIT.

5 And Goal

Something that has been very helpful for me is to make a list of five actions that I can take the very next day that will move me closer to my goal. This is not a to-do list like: take clothes to laundry, go to the bank, take kids to school, clean the house, etc. When you make your list and review it, ask yourself, "If I complete this item, will I be moving closer to my goal?" If the answer is yes, then it stays on your list. If the answer is no, then think of something else you can do to move yourself closer to your goal and put that item on the list. These should be actions that do not depend on other people. For example, when you write "Get a referral from Mary for my new business," you are depending on Mary to give you a referral in order for you to have completed or taken that action. Instead, write "Call/email Mary to ask her for a referral for my new business." This action depends only on you.

To make this even more impactful, you can prioritize the items on your list. Your first item should be the one which will move you closer toward your goal in a more significant way; then list each additional item in order of importance. Tackle the highest priority item first. This will ensure that even if you only get that one item checked off for the day, you will have made significant progress and will be moving closer to what you want to accomplish. By practicing this, I found that my days were very productive, and I was moving closer to my goal. When you do it, you will also be moving closer to your goal. Taking consistent action every day builds momentum and confidence towards what you are on your way to accomplishing.

> Taking consistent action every day builds momentum and confidence towards what you are on your way to accomplishing.

This is taking 100% responsibility; once again, recognize that making excuses or blaming something outside of yourself for your lack of results or failure to take action is unproductive. As Yoda would say, "Don't try. Do!" You create your own reality. The journey is the best part, and your journey will be unique; you will become who you have to become in the process.

Pay Attention To Feedback And Adjust

As you progress in your journey, you will inevitably run into positive and negative feedback. Pay attention to the feedback and use it to your advantage. Let's say your goal was to reduce your weight, and you were following a weight reduction plan to accomplish this goal. You ate the foods recommended, you did the exercise routine, and two weeks later you discover you have gained five pounds. Your initial reaction might be, "Wow! After all this sacrifice and discipline, I don't seem to be making any progress. This doesn't work." Examine the feedback and qualify it more carefully. What have you noticed? Do you feel heavier? Are your clothes feeling tight? Are people telling you that you look like you've gained a little weight? Or is it the opposite? Do you feel more energetic? Are your clothes feeling looser? Has anyone said you look slimmer? My mentor Jack Canfield says, "If one person calls you a horse, they are probably crazy; if five people call you a horse, it may be a conspiracy, but if 20 people call you a horse, then it might be time to buy a saddle."

Feedback allows you to assess whether you are going in the right direction or if we are off-course. As long as you take action, even if you get off course, paying attention to feedback helps you make adjustments and eventually get there.

Continue To Take Steps

Stop talking about what you are going to do and JUST DO IT! One step at a time, paying attention to feedback, adjusting your course, and continuing on your journey.

Chapter 3 Action Steps

"A journey of a thousand miles must begin with a single step."

Lao Tzu

1. Take the first step.
2. Divide into manageable actions.
3. Practice 5 and Goal.
4. Pay attention to feedback and adjust when needed.
5. Continue to take steps.

Chapter 4

Who's On Your Team?

> **"** *Lots of people want to ride with you in the limo, but what you want is someone who will take the bus with you when the limo breaks down."*
>
> **Oprah Winfrey**

When I was preparing to run the Chicago Marathon in 2006, there were many people that I considered to be on my team. There was my Coach Chewi, my parents, my family, my best friend Nel, my running club mates in 1427, my fellow runners that I saw while I trained at the central park, my future husband Antonio, whom I was just starting to get to know, and many others. The point is that when you set out to accomplish something big you need a team. A team to support you, encourage you, hold you accountable, and inspire you to get it done! How do you know who is right for your team?

The best people to have on your team are those that believe in you and what you are doing. If you are not sure if a person believes in you and what you are doing, just ask. Ask: "What do you think of this goal I want to accomplish?" Wait for the answer. If the answer is, "I think you are crazy. Why would you want to do such a thing? You will never be able to do that," then this is not a person you want on your team. Actually, this is not a person that you want to spend too much time with…period! This is what I consider a Dream Stealer. Dream Stealers are those people who, because they are not willing to do what is necessary to change their circumstances and create the life of their dreams, are not willing to let anyone else do it either.

Now if the answer is, "I think it is a great goal! How can I support you? I really believe you can achieve this, and I want to help," then this is a person whom you want to have on your team!

When it comes to those who will be in your corner, choose wisely. Make sure they are positive people who will bring a smile to your face when you think of them because they add value and positive energy to your life.

A Mentor Or Coach

My trainer Chewi's first marathon was the 2000 New York City Marathon. He told me that the reason he decided he wanted to run a marathon was that at the time here in Puerto Rico only elite runners ran marathons. So he wanted to test himself since he had already completed many half marathons. The way to get into the event was through a running club here on the island. His wife, at the time, got him the entry as a gift.

Since he didn't know any better, he had set his mind on running the marathon in three hours. He quickly learned from members of this club that there was some kind of myth or belief that it was not possible to run it in three hours. They told him he would not be able to do it and to just concentrate on finishing the race. Right then and there, he knew that even though these people would be accompanying him and participating along side him in the event, they really were not on his team.

He relied on his coach and trainer Sammy Laureano with whom he ran. Sammy was an elite runner who had just graduated in physiology and was starting to train other runners to improve their performance and increase their enjoyment of the sport. Chewi completely trusted him and followed everything he told him to do in order to prepare to run his first marathon in three hours.

Your Inner Circle

Earlier, I mentioned the importance of sharing your goal with your inner circle. Chewi has observed that one of the biggest obstacles

Make your inner circle part of your team.

people have when they set an important goal which requires time and sacrifice to achieve, is that they fail to share it with the people that are closest to them. They start to take the action towards achieving this goal, and then their spouse, friends and children start to complain or try to distract them from achieving it. This happens primarily because they were not made part of the team.

This shows the importance of sharing your goal, especially with those people that you want to have in your corner and that you interact with on a daily basis. It will make achieving your goal much easier and enjoyable. Explain to them what is involved, specifically the time commitment. If you must constantly justify the actions you are taking towards your goals, it will become increasingly more difficult for you to continue to take them. In extreme cases it could create an ultimatum, "it's your goal, or me!"

This is a dynamic which can be completely avoided, as long as you share your intentions and desires to accomplish your chosen goal with those closest to you.

There are some negative people that are energy suckers. These are the people you want to be wary of because they may think they have your best interest at heart, but in reality they are always thinking about themselves. You can probably think of a few people like this in your life. Some of these energy suckers may even be part of your family. So how do you avoid them? It's easy if they are not family, just don't spend any time with them. If they are family, then make sure you limit the amount of time you spend with them. You'll be glad you did.

> "You are the average of the five people you spend the most time with."
>
> **Jim Rohn**

As Jim Rohn says, "You are the average of the five people you spend the most time with." This is why you will want to have people on your team that are further ahead than you, to help you gain the skills and knowledge you need to accomplish your goal. A mentor or a coach would fit this criterion. You can also find a mentor by reading about the successes of others and by interacting with people who have already achieved the thing that you want to achieve. These people will not only serve as guides, but also as inspiration. When you learn from others who have achieved the same goal, it encourages and motivates you to continue to take the necessary actions to accomplish the same for yourself.

An Accountability Partner

It always helps to have an accountability partner on your team. This is someone with whom you will share your proposed actions for the day and will commit to them that you will get those actions done. They will do the same for you, and you will hold each other accountable for taking the actions. This works best when you have a consistent schedule to get together. Be it daily, once a week, every other day, etc. The important thing is for you to be meeting with regular frequency in order for it to be more effective for both of you.

When I was training for the marathon, my accountability partner was my coach. He would send out my training schedule the week before, and in order for me to receive the following week's schedule I had to send him what I had done for the week. This was his way of holding me accountable. If I did not report back to him, he would not send me my next training schedule. It worked! I knew if I wanted to know what to do next, I had to send him my results, even if it meant letting him know that I had missed a few days. Also, because he was my coach, he used my results to adjust my training accordingly. It was a form of feedback.

Your accountability partner can be a great person to ask for feedback and to brainstorm with for new ideas. When Antonio and

I were planning our first half day workshop in Puerto Rico, we came up with over 30 different names for it. I shared some of these possible names with my accountability partner Denny, and he actually gave me a great name that ended up becoming the one we decided to use. And thus was born, "Ignite Your Success," our workshop brand. My accountability partners have been invaluable to me, not only to keep me on track and moving forward towards my goals, but also by providing me with great ideas and feedback.

A Master Mind Group

A Master Mind group is a group of people who decide they want to meet on a regular basis and help each other with resources, feedback, ideas and support in general for achieving a specific goal or a number of them. In Napoleon Hill's classic book, *Think and Grow Rich*, he describes the power of the Master Mind as: "The coordination of knowledge and effort, in a spirit of harmony, between two or more people, for the attainment of a definite purpose." There are different formats for masterminding. You can meet in person, over the phone, on Skype or Google Hangout. If you prefer to meet in person, then you can look for people in your community who are interested in having accountability and more than one set of eyes, ears, and brains looking at a situation or goal from different angles to be able to achieve it more quickly and with less effort.

My mastermind group at the time when I was training for my marathon was comprised of people from my business and industry. None of them were runners or wanting to run a marathon. That did not take away from the value of the experience for me.

They were very supportive and even inspired by my goal and my progress towards it.

Since running my marathon, I have formed and participated in a number of different Master Mind groups, each with different purposes and modalities. I am currently part of a Master Mind where we are all transformational coaches and speakers, and we use the space to share ideas and experiences so we can all grow and become better within our own niches. This has allowed me to share ideas I am working on, get feedback, share my progress towards my current goals, and find solutions to obstacles I come across on my journey to where I want to go. Even better than that is the opportunity to help others in their own journey.

What I have found which ensures that the Master Mind is a valuable experience for all members is to follow the protocol you agree to during all meetings. This way everyone will be giving and getting something each time you meet. If this is something you want to learn more about, you can access more information in the resources section at the end of the book.

Others Wanting To Achieve Your Same Goal

Your peers and running mates are also an important part of your team. These are others who you either already know, or who you have met during your journey who are striving to achieve the same thing. My fellow jogger's club members were my peers and also running mates. During the marathon all the other participants were part of my team, and I was part of theirs as well. I knew if I needed encouragement I could count on them, and they knew they could count on me, too.

If you are taking that language class, then your fellow classmates are also learning to speak this new language. If you are working on getting to your target weight and have joined a gym, it would be your fellow gym members. In other words, everyone you encounter who is also working on achieving the same goal as you is part of your team.

Your Rocks

Some important members of your team are those people who will be there for you when the going gets tough. Usually these are the people who are willing to do the hard thing with you when necessary and not just enjoy the good stuff. We all have these friends whom are always present for the party and the glam and the glitz, then when you ask them to help you with a move or something not so glamorous, they are nowhere to be found.

My husband, Antonio, and I have moved a few times, and it is always interesting when this time comes because Antonio will still ask some of our friends for assistance. Believe it or not, a few agree and say they will be there. When the day comes, the one person who never fails us is our friend Gustavo. He has helped carry our big screen T.V. up and down a couple flights of stairs, loaded a small elevator with countless heavy items, and helped carry a very heavy Bar-B-Q up and down the two flights only to have to discard it since it had completely rusted from ocean-salt corrosion. He even brought a friend to help! We know from these experiences that we can always count on him for important things, even if they are not so glamorous and fun.

> Identify your rocks.

For something as important as your goal, you want to have the friends whom are willing to get their hands dirty in your corner. They will be there to encourage you during challenging times, and because they believe in you and what you are doing, they will make sure you keep on keeping on even when you might feel discouraged. I refer to these people as rocks. You can always count on them no matter what. They have your back in every situation.

Your Cheerleaders

You also really need to have cheerleaders and fans. People who are wanting to know about your progress and will be cheering you on every step of the way. These are people who usually want to help you achieve your goal and will offer to pitch in and maybe even have friends who may make your journey quicker and easier. The more you share your vision with others, the more opportunities and individuals you will be exposed to, which may make your goal easier to achieve.

Possibility Channels And Dead Ends

Has anyone ever shared something with you which he or she wanted to achieve? What was your response to his or her desire and dream? Was your response discouraging? Or did you get excited and start thinking of ways you might be able to help make that dream a reality? This is a revealing question because it will let you know how you might be approaching life yourself. When you are encouraging and positive, you are acting as a possibility channel. When you are discouraging and negative, you are not a channel, but rather a dead end.

How can you become aware of who the possibility channels and energy suckers are in your life? Here's a quick way: Make a list of all the people with whom you spend a significant amount of time. This list can include friends, people at work, family members, church members, and people from your gym or other organizations. Make sure they are people whom you interact with at least once a week for more than 30 minutes.

Next, go through your list, and next to each name put either a plus (+) or a minus sign(-). Put a (+) next to the names of people who you feel are adding value to your life because they make you smile, are encouraging, positive, and who you look forward to seeing. Put a (-) next to names of people who you feel are negative, discouraging, prone to complain endlessly, or who blame you or others inappropriately. Do the same for those people who make you feel like the life has been sucked out of you when you spend time with them, those people that you do not enjoy interacting with for whatever reason. The names with the (+) next to them are your possibility channels, while the others are your dead ends and energy suckers.

I remember the first time I did this exercise, I was pleasantly surprised by the fact that I had already "cleaned house," so to speak, with regards to spending time with certain people. The eye opener for me occurred when I did this exercise again about 18 months later and discovered there were a few people on the list who I originally thought were possibility channels, and who had turned into dead ends and energy suckers. This is why I would suggest you do this exercise at least once a year, especially if you are working on yourself and growing. When I did this, I was a very different person from the year before, and you will be, too!

Go To The "Bellagio"

When it comes to managing your time, spend the least amount of time with the dead ends and energy suckers. Sometimes, you'll be unable to limit the amount of time you spend with them. In cases like this, you can do one of the following things to block their negative energy. Before you meet with them, imagine yourself surrounded by a wall of water similar to the fountains at the Bellagio Hotel in Las Vegas. If you haven't been there, it is a sight to see, and may be a place you want to add to your list of 101 goals. In the meantime, you can find a picture of them by doing a search on Google Images for "Bellagio Fountains." The other thing you can do, by itself or combined with the wall of water, is to imagine yourself surrounded by a field of bright, white light. This will protect you from their negative energy.

My husband and I do this a lot. In fact, if we are in a situation where one of us perceives an energy sucker, we will say to each other "let's go to the Bellagio." That is our signal to put up the wall of water and to become immune to their negativity.

Who wants to be on the same team as someone with dead end thinking? No one does! I know this is not you because the fact that you are reading this book says you are looking for possibilities and more options in your life. When we hear the dreams and goals of others, it is only natural for us to want to help. Share your vision, especially with those whom believe in you and care about you. It will start a shift, not only in them but in the universe to put things, people, and circumstances in front of you to help you get to where you want go.

Chapter 4 Action Steps

"There is no such thing as a self made man. You will reach your goals only with the help of others."

George Shinn

1. Find a mentor or coach (if you don't have one already).
2. Share your vision and goal with your inner circle (spouse, children, close friends) and explain to them what is involved in your achieving this goal.
3. Get an accountability partner.
4. Form or join a Master Mind Group.
5. Identify others wanting to achieve your same goal or something similar.
6. Identify your rocks.
7. Share your vision to identify your cheerleaders.
8. Identify your possibility channels and your dead ends.
9. Go to the "Bellagio" when you encounter energy suckers.

Chapter 5

See Yourself Crossing
the Finish Line

"*Imagination is everything. It is the preview of life's coming attractions.***"**

Albert Einstein

Did you know that your mind cannot tell the difference between a real experience and a vividly imagined one? Well, it's true. Many athletes and high-performing people know this as fact. One of the first to use the technique of visualization to accomplish goals was Wallace D. Wattles. He describes it in his book *The Science of Getting Rich*. This book was originally published in 1910, and I have read it many times and truly believe in, and practice, the techniques described within it. Several athletes and top performers practice this to increase their level of performance and to take their goals and life to the next level.

When I was training for the Chicago Marathon, this was something I did during every one of my training sessions. As I was coming towards the end of the session, I would visualize myself crossing the finish line strong as I had done in previous shorter distance races like the 10k's. I did a lot of my long runs in the mountains here in Puerto Rico in a town named Jajome in the city of Cayey. There is a route that is measured and labeled on the road up to six miles. Many runners use this route for training for longer distance races like the half and full marathons. The distance you want to run determines how far you will go on the route. For example, if my long run was a 16 mile run I would run up to the five mile marker and back, which would be 10 miles; then, I would run out to the three mile marker and back for the remaining six miles.

Returning to the starting point of this route is spectacular! The last mile has beautiful views of the Caribbean Sea to your left, and you can feel and breathe the fresh mountain air as you are making your way back to your car as you finish your training for the day. This image is one which I use often when I am training for current races; it's inspiring and motivating, and my body knows exactly how much more I have to run before crossing the finish line, as I imagine myself looking down at the Caribbean Sea from the Jajome hills in Cayey.

Many athletes practice this. In a video by the Washington Post on swimmer and Olympic gold medalist Michael Phelps, the most decorated Olympian to date with 22 medals, visualization was highlighted as an important part of his training. In this video, Phelps and his coach Bob Bowman discuss how important visualization has been for his success and confidence. Phelps has visualized himself swimming the perfect race over and over again. He visualized this perfect race from different angles and with different scenarios. He visualized himself in the water, from the stands, and even imagined scenarios of "what if it doesn't go perfectly." He mentioned things like his swimsuit tearing or his goggles breaking. Visualizing these different scenarios and what he would do in each of them created a database in his brain so in the event any of these became a reality in his actual race, he would know exactly what to do and how. This practice of not only visualizing the perfect race but imagining the things that could go wrong, gave him the confidence in knowing that he had a plan for whatever would come.

I recently put this to the test once more in a bit of a different way. I was registered to run the Divas half marathon here in Puerto Rico on November 11, 2012, after being on vacation from running since the Buenos Aires half marathon in September 2011. I had been training somewhat consistently since the end of August. I was feeling really good by the beginning of October and was running six miles in about an hour. I became sick with some kind of flu towards the end of October and was literally home in bed for over a week. I could not remember the last time I had gotten so sick. Needless to say, I was not running. I thought to myself, "Here we go again; another year of not running the Divas half here in Puerto Rico." I had not been able to run the year before due to some scheduling conflicts. I had accepted the fact it was not going to happen, especially since I had not finished my training. A half marathon is 13.1 miles, and the most I had run since September of the previous year was six miles.

The day before the marathon I was feeling really good and back to about 95% of my healthy self. I told my husband, "Let's go pick up my race packet; I want to run the race." So we did. I decided to run it fully aware of the fact that I had not trained properly and that I would more than likely have to walk a great portion of the route. I did it! It was not very glamorous, as I did mostly walk after mile eight. I completed the half marathon in just under three hours. Not my best time indeed! The time really did not matter to me; the important thing is that I had made a commitment to myself when I originally registered for the event and knew that if I was feeling good and did not run it I would forever ask myself why I didn't run it.

There was a consequence to my running the event without proper training. My ankle started to bother me the week after the race and became very swollen and tender. I was out of commission; no running for me. But wait, I was registered for the Miami half marathon on January 27, 2013. I rested for two weeks and then made an attempt to run. It was a no go. My ankle bothered me right away. There I was about two months from the next race, and I was not able to physically run. I had finished writing the first version of this chapter a few weeks before and I thought "How interesting. It's time to put this to the test in a different way." I had always used visualization during my training sessions when I was physically doing the activity. This time I would do it without actually doing the physical activity.

My husband was also training for the Miami race. Every time he would kiss me goodbye to go for his run I would think to myself "another day of non-running. I think this time I will be a cheerleader at the marathon rather than a participant." One day I told him I was going to start training with him… in my mind. "Great experiment," he said. So before he went for his run, I would ask him how far he was running and what route he was taking. I would then lie or sit listening to my running music on my iPod while closing my eyes, and imagining myself running from our house, down the street, continuing through the entire route, and returning back to our house.

It was so much fun! I would see all the buildings, nature, even people walking or sitting at one of the sidewalk cafes I would pass on my run. The interesting thing was that I asked Antonio how long it took him to run the route; it happened to be within five minutes of the time it took me to visualize myself running the same route in my mind. I did this for the entire month of December. On December 31st, I started running again physically. That first week I ran up to six miles during one training session. Two weeks before the half marathon in Miami, I ran 10 miles for the first time since the Divas event; then the weekend before the big day, I got in another 10 mile run. I was ready for Miami.

> Visualizing not only works for athletic performance, it also works for learning new skills and for accelerating the achievement of your goals.

I ran Miami with three weeks of physical running and eight weeks of mental running. My time for running the race in Miami was two hours and twenty one minutes, which is six minutes slower than when I ran it in 2011 with a full three months of training. I finished feeling so awesome and excited! I felt like I could run another 13 miles! I attribute this to my visualization practice for this event and my expectation for the best.

Visualizing not only works for athletic performance, it also works for learning new skills and for accelerating the achievement of your goals. There was a study done by a professor in Neurology in Harvard where they had a group of volunteers, none of whom knew how to play the piano or type with all fingers. The first group would go to a room with a piano in it and be given five finger exercises to perform on the piano. The second group would also spend the same amount of time in the room and would not touch the piano or be given any instructions on what to practice. The third group was given the instructions on performing the exercises and only did them mentally. They could touch the piano but not move their fingers. Here are the results:

- Group 1: Showed growth in the motor cortex area of the brain that governs the movement of the fingers.
- Group 2: Showed no change in brain activity.
- Group 3: Showed an almost identical amount of growth in the area of the brain governing the fingers as did the first group (Pascual-Leone 315)

This study showed that visualization and imagination have a real physical effect on the brain. It also showed that a combination of physical practice and mental practice can yield the best performances.

So how do you visualize? Visualization is the practice of seeing yourself in your mind's eye being, doing, and having the things that you want with vivid detail and emotion. You may be thinking you're really not a good visualizer. This can seem like a difficult task. Have you ever had a really vivid dream that seemed so real until you woke up? Visualizing is like having a very vivid dream that you are creating with your conscious mind. The practice of visualization stimulates your sub-conscious mind and it's creativity. It opens your conscious mind up to new awarenesses and opportunities regarding the thing you are visualizing, be it something positive or negative.

> Visualizing is like having a very vivid dream that you are creating with your conscious mind.

Have you noticed when you see something new, something which you have "never" seen before, it begins to appear over and over again? The reality is that most of the time it was already there; you were just not focusing on it, so you did not "see" it. This is what visualization can do for you. Once you see yourself clearly being, having, and doing what you want successfully, you will become aware of things, opportunities, and people whom can help you make your goal a reality.

While, it is important to have high intentions regarding your goals, at the same time, having low attachment to the outcome is a good approach. What this means is to not get so attached to a specific outcome, as to close yourself off to other possibilities or something better. When you set your intentions for what you want or something better, you open up an unlimited supply of possibilities and experiences to achieve the thing you want.

Practice Visualizing

You can start to practice by visualizing things which are familiar to you. Let's say your car or your kitchen or your favorite dress. Close your eyes and imagine walking into your kitchen. What color is the countertop? What is it made of? What about your refrigerator? Walk over to the cabinets and open one of the doors and take something out. What is it? How does it feel? This is a simple exercise you can do to develop your visualization skills.

Write Your Ideal Scene

If you haven't written out an ideal scene of you accomplishing your goal yet, now is the time to do it. This can be very helpful in your visualization practice. Write out what you would be doing, what you would be seeing, smelling, hearing and feeling with as much detail as you can imagine. A great way to ensure that you are being detailed enough is to ask the question "How can I be more specific?" after you read your description of you accomplishing your goal. This will give you more ideas for details for your vision. For example, if you are visualizing yourself living in your dream home, start by asking "How can I be more specific? Where is this dream home? What country? What state? What city? What street? What number is it? What color is it? How many bedrooms? What does the furniture look like? Is it leather? Is it wood? Metal? What view do you see out your window? What are you wearing? What do you smell? What do you hear? How are you feeling in your dream home? Who is there with you?" I could go on and on with questions. The answers are in the questions, so keep asking yourself the questions to create your ideal vision. Expect the best outcome in your vision.

> The answers are in the questions.

A very important part of visualization is belief. If you are visualizing something and you do not believe it to be possible, then you are trumping the whole process. In the movie *Star Wars Episode V: The Empire Strikes Back*, there is a great scene that illustrates this. Luke is training with Master Yoda in the use of "the force;" he is able to levitate rocks the size of a soccer ball. His spaceship, which had landed in a swampy area, starts to sink until it is completely under water.

Yoda: "You can use the force to lift your ship."
Luke: "It is too big."
Yoda: "You just have to focus; size does not matter."
Yoda lifts the ship using "the force" and Luke says, "I can't believe it."
Yoda: "That is why you fail."

If you do not believe it is possible, it is the equivalent of planning to fail. Our thoughts are so powerful that if you think you can or think you can't, either way you are right! So why not choose the positive alternative which is that you can?

> Our thoughts are so powerful that if you think you can or think you can't, either way you are right!

For me, it was very inspiring to learn of others who had succeeded at accomplishing my goal, yet they would seem to have every excuse for not achieving it. When I accompanied my running group to Boston in early 2006, I was at the expo when I met a father and son team who were running the Boston Marathon that year for the 25th time!

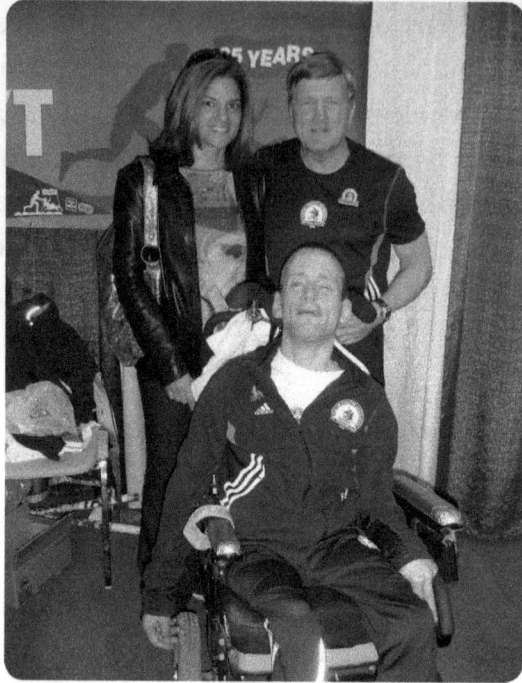

Team Hoyt at Boston Marathon Expo 2006

That wasn't what was so inspiring about them. This was a 60-something year old father who ran the marathon pushing his 40-some year old quadriplegic son in his wheelchair for the full 26.2 miles! WOW! I am talking about Team Hoyt. I thought if he has run this marathon over 20 times while pushing his son, why wouldn't I be able to do it? After all, I was not only younger, I also wasn't exerting the extra effort to push someone or something for the whole distance. Team Hoyt has not only completed the Boston Marathon over 25 times, they have participated in many other races.

One of the most incredible accomplishments they have achieved is the Iron Man Triathlon, which consists of a 2.4 mile swim, a 112 mile bicycle ride and then a 26.2 mile run. Dick Hoyt swam 2.4 miles with a raft attached to his waist that carried his son Rick. He then carried his son in his arms and placed him on a special seat on the front of his bike and rode 112 miles. Then he carried him off the bike into his special wheelchair and pushed him while running for 26.2 miles to finish the event. What an inspiration they are! They helped me believe that I could also accomplish this. Believe you CAN and you WILL.

Create A Vision Board Or Goals Book

Some tools that can help you see yourself accomplishing your goal are creating a vision board or a goals book with pictures. A vision board is like a poster which has images and words that represent the goals and vision you have for your life. If you saw the movie The Secret, Jon Assaraf mentions it during his intervention. He used vision boards to visualize and focus daily on the things he wanted to be, do, and have, and as a way of continuously being in a state of already having achieved them. He attributes many of the goals he has achieved to this practice.

See yourself accomplishing your goal.

A goals book is similar to a vision board except that you write your goals and collect pictures that represent them in a book format. It's like a scrapbook of your goals. A great thing to do is to take a picture of yourself doing the thing that you want to accomplish. If your goal was to own a Corvette, you could go to the car dealership and ask for a test drive and have the salesperson take a picture of you behind the wheel of your dream car. The test drive will give you the feeling and experience of already having achieved your goal, and the picture will give you a visual image you can use for your vision board or goals book.

If you are unable to physically create a situation, you can still create it using Google Images. Let's say your goal is to have a baby. You can find a picture of a pregnant woman on Google Images. Simply print the picture and paste your face over the image. Now you can use this picture and put it on your vision board or in your goals book and look at it daily as many times as possible. You may also want to put this picture in a strategic place in your home, like on your bathroom mirror, on your refrigerator door, your desk, in your car, in your wallet, etc. This can serve as a frequent daily reminder.

I created a mini video of my goals and affirmations which I could listen to or watch on my iPhone. I took the same images that I had used to create my vision board and added a written affirmation for each goal. I did this in the form of a slide show. I used video editing software to add relaxing background music and recorded myself saying my affirmations out loud while the appropriate slide was on the screen. I had it repeat itself four times. The total duration of it was close to 16 minutes. If I viewed or listened to it only once, it was under four minutes. This gave me an easy flexible way to review and visualize daily. After I had viewed it a number of times, I could just listen to the audio and see the pictures in my mind.

Visualize Daily

Now that you have a movie-like description of you being, doing, and having your goal, you need to prepare to visualize it. It is very important to put yourself in a relaxed state before you visualize so that you are tapping into your sub-conscious mind. To relax yourself, start by slowing down your breathing. A way to do this is to breathe in four counts and breathe out six to eight counts. As you concentrate on your breath, you can say "relax" silently to yourself. You can breathe in "re" and breathe out "lax." Next, consciously relax each part of your body, starting with the top of your head and working down to the soles of your feet. Release any tension that is being held in your body and relax your muscles.

Let's clear your mind now. If you are still saying the "relax" mantra, this can help in clearing and quieting your mind. This part takes practice. You will find thoughts popping in here and there, and the best thing to do is to just observe them as if the thought was a boat floating down a river. Just remember to resist the temptation to jump into the boat! Let them float on by as you refocus on your vision. Once you have done this, you are ready to visualize.

It is very important that you visualize yourself in the present moment because if you are visualizing yourself in the future your vision will remain in the future and out of reach. Your goal with visualization is to engage all your senses. What would you be hearing, touching, smelling, tasting? Engage your emotions. What would you be feeling? Gratitude? Peace? Love? Joy? See yourself in motion like watching a movie of you in the experience of achieving your goal. YES! YOU DID IT! This practice has a big impact even though it takes very little time!

Chapter 5 Action Steps

"Whatever the mind can conceive and believe it can achieve."

Napoleon Hill

1. Practice visualizing (start with something familiar).
2. Write out your ideal scene with every detail and incorporate all senses and feelings (remember to be very specific).
3. Create a Vision Board or Goals Book.
4. Visualize daily (see yourself in the present moment achieving your goal).

Chapter 6

And the Gun Goes Off!

"_You don't have to be great to start, but you have to start to be great._"

Zig Ziglar

I will never forget that October morning. The 22nd, 2006 in downtown Chicago. It was 46 degrees and drizzling. I am a freeze baby, so I went ready to face the cold. I had my leggings, long sleeve top, singlet over that, a paper jacket over that, and a fleece hoodie on top of all of those. Oh, and gloves and a running hat, too. I even had a disposable camera, so I could document my experience. It was the 29th running of the Chicago Marathon, and most importantly to me, it was my FIRST MARATHON.

On my four and a half hour flight over from San Juan, I spent some time writing in my journal. Besides writing down my thoughts and feelings as I approached the big day, I wrote down the names of the people or groups of people whom I was dedicating each mile to and why. I had heard of others who had done this and decided that it would make my experience more meaningful if I did this as well. The night before the race, I transferred the list of people from my journal on to a numbered piece of paper. I then made cuts into the strip, so I could tear each name off as I completed each mile on my journey. I pinned this list to my bib number.

My Bib Number With the Numbered Strip of Paper Attached

After four months of training, I was finally there, waiting for the starting gun to go off. I prepared in the usual way: turning on my foot pod, setting my watch to be ready for crossing the start line, turning my MP3 player on, etc. My watch went blank; my MP3 player did not power on (in spite of having charged it all night)! I thought "WOW! Now what?" I had always run with music. I was able to get my watch ready through a reset, although not on the correct date. My MP3 player was a mystery, or was it? I looked down at my bib number, saw my first mile dedication, looked up and nodded. Of course! This was supposed to be a different experience for me...

BANG! The gun went off, and I was running among 40,000 other people. It was very exciting! I had dedicated the first mile of the marathon to God, for giving me the strength and courage to follow my own dreams and desires. This, I believe, had everything to do with the rest of my journey...

Chicago Marathon Runners 2006

What was so amazing was that with each and every mile, I visualized myself running with the person or group of people for whom I had dedicated it to. Memories of things they had taught me or experiences we had shared together would fill my thoughts, and the experience was completely different than any I had ever encountered. The absence of my go-to props made it much more significant. There was a magical moment during the race as I was mentally running the seventh mile with my paternal grandmother Mami Ruth and remembering times with her and my father's family, and how she showed me how to have fun in life. She was in a nursing home at the time, and it was very hard for me to visit her and see her because I wanted to remember her in her lively full-of-life days. During this mile, I was compelled at one point to look to my right—I was running past a nursing home and all the elderly people were looking through the window waving with signs that read "GO RUNNERS," "YOU CAN DO IT!" It is an image I will never forget...

Chewi's Story

There he was in New York City the day before his first marathon alone without his wife and kids. He did have two of his brothers there for support. There was a pre-event United Nations Race where all the flags of the different participating countries were being paraded around a five mile course. Chewi saw that the runner carrying the Puerto Rican flag could hardly handle the weight of it, let alone the physical challenge of running with it. He ran up next to him and said, "Are you doing okay there?" Then, he grabbed the flag and ran like a madman with it.

He thought, up until then, it was the fastest three miles he had ever run. He was so excited to be there in New York to run for the first time outside of Puerto Rico! Everyone from his running club asked: "What have you done? You just threw your race for tomorrow!" Remember, he did not really pay much attention to these people, as they had proven to him they did not have much faith in him.

He was a little nervous about not having run in such cool temperatures before. He literally tried on countless running outfits, and ran outside to see which one he would finally wear the day of the event. After his run-away fashion show, he went with a singlet, shorts, a paper jacket and a winter cap to keep his head warm.

It was 40 degrees on race day in New York City. Over 30,000 participants waited anxiously for the gun to go off! Chewi stood there. The only thing making him anxious being the pressure he was putting on himself to finish the race in less than three hours. Bang! He was off with the rest of the pack of runners focused on his goal!

Show Up!

Show Up!

Now that you have done your due diligence and prepared for the main event, the next step is to SHOW UP! This may seem obvious, but you would be surprised how sometimes it is not so obvious and we let things get in the way of accomplishing our goal. Have you ever made a commitment and when the time came for you to make good on it, you came up with excuses to let yourself off the hook? This is the same as not showing up.

Greg's Story

My friend Greg had set a goal to run the Chicago Marathon in 2009. Antonio and I said we would do it as well. Greg is a crane operator in the city of Chicago, and sometimes he can be away on a job for weeks. He had done all the training really well, up until about a couple of months before the marathon when it became nearly impossible for him to run enough.

About two weeks before the marathon my friend Kellie, Greg's wife, sent me a text message. She mentioned that Greg was saying he was not going to run because he had not trained enough. I thought, "Oh no! I have to call and encourage him." I called him and said with excitement, "I can't wait to see you and be at the starting line on Marathon Sunday! Kellie told me you were talking about not running. What are you thinking?" He proceeded to tell me how he had not trained enough and didn't think he would make it. I said, "Greg, did you think you were going to win this thing? All you have to do is finish! You can do it, even if you have to walk some of the way. The important thing is that you do it! Imagine how you are going to feel if Antonio and I cross the finish line and you don't run. You'll say to yourself, 'I should have done it, too!' You don't want that? Do you? You want to cross the finish line with us and say to yourself , 'I am so glad I did!'"

> You want to cross the finish line with us and say to yourself, 'I am so glad I did!'

In the very moment when you are considering not showing up, you should ask yourself what it will cost you not to show up on the day you are to complete your goal. And more important, ask what you will gain by showing up and getting it done.

Pace Yourself!

The euphoria, adrenaline, and anticipation of the participants' desire to finish during my first marathon was contagious and even a little dangerous at times. When you approach the starting line for your goal, this can happen to you as well. This is why it is important to pace yourself. As in a marathon, you don't want to start out too fast because you may run out of steam and not have enough energy to get to the finish line.

Antonio's Story

My husband told me about his experience during his first marathon, which just happened to be the 2005 Chicago Marathon. He had set a goal to run the 26.2 miles in 03:15:00, but the day before the marathon, his friend told him that if he ran it in 03:10:00, he would qualify for the Boston Marathon the following year. As the oldest and one of the most prestigious events in the United States, you have to qualify by running a half marathon or marathon within a certain time in order to participate in the Boston Marathon. Only 20,000 participants can run, which is half of the number of participants in Chicago and other major races. So, Antonio decided to attempt to make the run in 03:10:00.

The day of the marathon Antonio ran with the pacers (participants that volunteer to help other participants pace their race to do it in a certain time). He ran with them until the 10k mark, which is six miles into the race. There were still 20 more miles to go. He was so excited by all the people running, and he felt so good that he decided to pick up the pace because he thought and felt that they were going too slow.

At mile 16 he started to pay for not pacing himself in the beginning. His feet started to hurt, then his calves, and he had to slow down. When he got to mile 20 his knees really hurt a lot, and he did not know if he was going to make it. He started to walk during mile 21, and during the next mile the pacers passed him by. When they passed him he said to himself, "Okay. Now is the time," and he started to run with them again but couldn't keep up. What seemed so slow to him at the beginning was now a huge challenge. They kept getting further ahead of him, until halfway through mile 23 when he couldn't see them anymore.

With only 2.2 miles to go, he said to himself, "Okay. You only have two more little miles to go." Those were the two longest miles of his life; it seemed like he was never going to get to the finish line. He finally made it! Even though he did not make his desired time, he finished in 03:14:29. Just under his original goal of 03:15:00!

The really neat thing about this story is that about two months after the marathon Antonio's friend called him and asked, "How old are you?" "34," said Antonio. "When is your birthday?" asked his friend. Antonio said "I will be 35 on February 18th." His friend started to scream excitedly and told him "YOU QUALIFIED FOR BOSTON!"

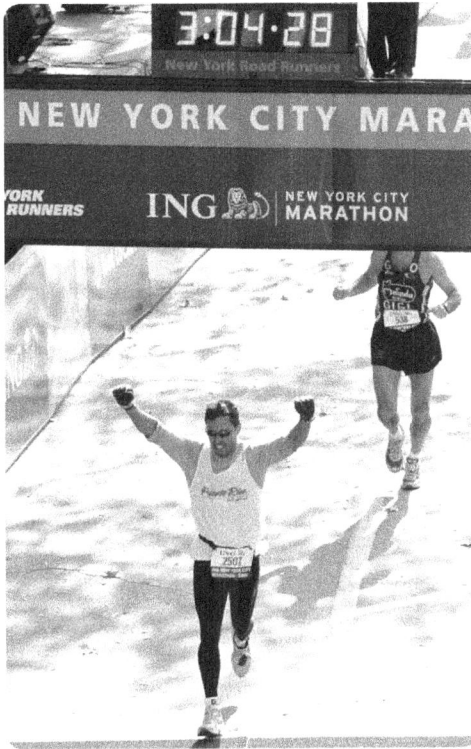

Antonio Crossing the Finish Line of the New York City Marathon in 2006

The time he made at the Chicago Marathon was the qualifying time for the age group of 35—40 year olds. The age that counted was the age you would be on the day of the marathon. Pacing yourself can help you avoid de-

Pacing yourself can help you avoid delays on your journey further down the road, and also make the journey less painful.

lays on your journey further down the road, and also make the journey less painful.

If You Have A False Start, Start Again!

There are pitfalls other than pacing that you should consider. Over-excitement can also lead to a false start. In sports, this can have a very big impact, as it can mean being disqualified in the event, or receiving a penalty. In life, a false start can occur when you start a job and decide a few days later that it's not what you want to do.

This happened recently to me in my dental practice. My partner was retiring, and I wanted to find another dentist to take her place. I spoke to a colleague to ask for ideas on finding a dentist, and she spoke to a resident that worked with her. The resident called me, and we had an interview. I described the type of clinic that we have. We see patients by appointment with each appointment having specific procedures scheduled for it. I explained that we are an esthetic dentistry practice with a spa-like environment where we like to pamper our patients. I explained we are not a high-volume practice, but rather a high quality service practice. It seemed we had a really good fit and that she would allow us to offer some additional treatment options which we were currently referring out.

We had to delay her official starting date as she had some challenges with our local Health Department and the paper work for her state dental license. The person who had to sign it was on vacation, so we set her start date for August after returning from our yearly summer recess. Three days after she started, she met with me and told me that she did not think it was going to work out for her in our practice. She had received calls from other dentists that had high-volume clinics, and she felt that at this time in her career these clinics might be a better fit. I agreed with her. This ended up being a false start for her in her goal of working in a dental practice. Did she fail to accomplish her goal? No. Just the opposite. She is now working in a high-volume dental practice which ended up being a better fit for her. A false start is not the end of the world; the important thing is to just start again!

A false start is not the end of the world... the important thing is to just start again!

Enjoy The Journey; Expect To Succeed!

Remember the only way you can fail is to quit. So show up! You're ready for it! This is the moment you have been working towards, so be confident in your preparation no matter how much. This is the moment to keep the end goal in mind, see it clearly, and remind yourself of all the reasons you wanted to do it. Make sure you are enjoying the journey, pace yourself, expect to finish, and believe in yourself! I believe in you!

Chapter 6 Action Steps

"It is only the first step that is difficult."

Marie De Vichy-Chamrond

1. Show Up!
2. Pace yourself!
3. If you have a false start, start again!
4. Enjoy the journey; expect to finish; expect to succeed!

Chapter 7

Halfway There!

66 *We're only halfway to what we think we can achieve."*
Bill Gates

So far in the marathon I had run with God, my parents, my sisters Monica and Rosana, my brother-in-law Che, my two grandmothers, my girls Marianna and Danielle, my team from my business, my friend Enrique who introduced me to running, and my first coach Manuel, to whom I had dedicated mile 13.

The halfway mark of the marathon is 13.1 miles. This was a very exciting point in the race, and there was a huge banner that read "Halfway There!" WOW! To realize that I had run that far and that I was just about to do it all again! How awesome! I kept the end in mind and because I was running "with" different people during each mile, it never entered my mind to stop. I looked forward to each mile and the experience it would bring.

Celebrate; You Are Halfway There!

This can be both thrilling and overwhelming. For those of us who see the glass as half-full, we know we can fill it (or get to the finish line) because we have already gotten halfway there. For those of you who may see the glass as half-empty at times, it can seem very daunting to have to do it all again in order to get to where you want to go. This is the place in the process that you want to acknowledge yourself for what you have accomplished up to this point. Give yourself a high five! Make sure you are writing down your successes in your victory log. Focus on what you have done so far instead of what you still have to do. Remember that you can do it; you already have put forth half the effort, just put it forth again and you'll be there!

> Acknowledge yourself for what you have accomplished up to this point.

Halfway Point of the Chicago Marathon 2006

This is not the time to get comfortable and complacent. Imagine that you have been pushing a boulder up a hill and that your goal is to have it make it down the other side. If you get to the top and stop for air for too long, the boulder could start going back down the wrong side of the hill, and you would have to put in just as much effort if not more to get it back up. On the other hand, if you don't let up on the pressure and effort that you put on the boulder, it will get to the tipping point where it has gained enough force and momentum that it can be very difficult to stop.

When Antonio and I were preparing for our first "Ignite Your Success" workshop, our 10 year old son Antonio Anibal took out a Christmas present he had received from my best friend Nel. It was a 1000 piece puzzle. Yes! 1000 PIECES! He said to my husband, "Dad, I want to do this with you. Will you help me?" It was a Sunday, so there was time to work on the puzzle. They started working on it, and Antonio told our son "Let's get all the border pieces together, that way we can complete the puzzle border first." About 10 minutes into the activity, little Antonio lost interest, as he began to realize the size of the task they had just undertaken. My husband continued to put together the border, and as I walked by, I put in a piece here and there.

A few hours later, the border was finished, and I was now helping Antonio out. The puzzle featured a picture of the FIFA World Cup with all the flags of the participating countries in this international soccer federation. We had separated all the pieces by color, and each of us was working on a different one and in a different section of the puzzle. We ended up completing a little more than a quarter of it and decided it was time for bed; it was close to midnight.

Monday came around, and as I was preparing for our upcoming Saturday workshop, I couldn't help but spend a few minutes here and there on the puzzle. It was sitting on our coffee table in our living room, just behind where I have my office space set up in our home. Antonio came home for lunch, and once again, we found ourselves sitting in front of it. That evening the puzzle called us back for more; we literally went to bed at about 1 a.m.

As Tuesday's full schedule of my seeing patients and Antonio working his business loomed, we still needed to complete our final preparations for our workshop. We started on our presentation when ...you guessed it... the puzzle grabbed us like a magnet! We could not stay away. We could taste victory as the picture grew more and more complete minute by minute. We were not only working on our particular sections of the puzzle, we were now collaborating! "See if you can find the piece that is half green with a white tip and a black line going down the middle." Or, "I'm looking for a piece that is completely red except for one of its ears which is white." "I got it." This went on for hours until we were about 30—40 pieces from finishing. And surprise... it was close to 2 a.m.

We couldn't stop now. We had to finish! So we did! It was so awesome! We jumped up and down, high fived each other, took pictures of the puzzle and posted them on facebook. I mean this was a great accomplishment! ONE THOUSAND PIECES! YEAH!

Have a clear picture of what your end result will look like.

What kept us so enthralled while completing the project was that we had a clear picture of what the end result would look like. We had the box with the picture of the finished puzzle on it. It not only served as a clear objective, but also allowed us to assess where we were in our progress. At a glance, we could know more or less how much more we had to go. The desire to finish the puzzle before little Antonio was back at the house with us on our next weekend with the kids served to act as the "why" driving us to finish. My husband wanted to teach our son the importance of not giving up and the value of finishing what you start.

The 1000 Piece Puzzle Antonio and I Finished!

As in everything, there is a moment of critical mass, where once you arrive, there is a sort of snowball effect where you can move faster and with less effort to cover the same distance. When you are halfway to your goal, it is critical to keep moving forward. This is what will ensure that you have momentum on your side.

Rely On Your Team To Keep Your Momentum Going

Let's revisit Greg's story. Up until about two weeks from marathon day all Greg kept hearing from family and friends was "You can't do it. You don't know what you are doing. You are not built to run a marathon." Greg is 6'3" with a big bone body frame. He had some people on his team that were not really with him on his vision.

Remember how crucial this is when you want to achieve something important? After we spoke, he felt empowered and encouraged and was determined to "prove all these naysayers wrong."

So on October 11, 2009, on Marathon Sunday, our strategy was for all three of us to cross the finish line together. If we had to slow down or walk some of the way that was fine, as long as we kept going all the way to the finish. Greg thought he had run up to 12 miles during his training; however, the recommended training regimen for a marathon includes doing at least one 20 mile run before the big day.

We were off! We were all very excited and started running at a good pace. We passed the 5K mark, then the 10K mark. Yeah! We passed the 15K mark, and then we made it to the 21K mark (also known as "Halfway There." WOW! Our momentum was good, and the next couple of miles we kept our momentum in spite of the pain and fatigue starting to affect Greg. I could tell he was starting to feel the effects of the distance we had covered, as well as the fact that he hadn't run this far during his training. His body was going into unchartered territory. I said to him, "Let me know if you want to slow down." He said, "You don't have to stay with me. You guys can go ahead if you want." "No," we said, "we came here to run the whole thing with you, so if we need to slow down we will."

We slowed down as Greg's muscles were beginning to feel fatigued. We reached mile 15 and really started to high five and count down the miles. I would say, "Only 11 more miles to go, woo hoo!" We began to walk and run. As we got to mile 17 Greg was starting to have shooting pain from his ankle all the way up his legs. We told him we'd walk if we needed to walk, and with only nine more miles to go, we would do it together. Even though Greg was in pain, I could tell he was determined to finish and being there with him was instrumental to this.

This demonstrates the importance of having the right people on your team, people that are encouragers who will be with you when the going gets tough, who will walk through the fire to get to the other side with you. Having a group that believes in you can really help, especially if you come to a point where you are tired and maybe even starting to question what you are doing.

Running the Chicago Marathon with Greg (left)
and my husband Antonio (right) in 2009

Keep Taking Steps, Even If At A Slower Pace

In order to take advantage of momentum, it is important to choose to keep going, keep moving forward, even if at a slower pace. It is much harder to stop something that is in motion versus something that is not. As John C. Maxwell says "momentum is the great exaggerator." When you have momentum on your side, nothing seems to go wrong, challenges seem like no big deal and are easily handled, and pain and exhaustion remain in the background as our focus is on where we are going and how far we have come to get there.

Chapter 7 Action Steps

"It was character that got us out of bed, commitment that moved us into action, and discipline that enabled us to follow through."

Zig Ziglar

1. Celebrate your accomplishments; acknowledge that you are halfway there!
2. Rely on your team for encouragement and support to keep your momentum going.
3. Keep taking steps, even if you must slow your pace.

Chapter 8

Dig Deep!!!!

> 66 *You have to do what others won't. To achieve what others don't."*
>
> **Anonymous**

There is a moment during the marathon which runners refer to as "hitting the wall." This is usually around mile 20 of the course. The scientific explanation of "hitting the wall" or "bonking" is the depletion of glycogen stores in the muscles and liver. This causes you to basically run out of energy and thus hit the wall and want to stop or quit. Have you ever been very close to getting something or achieving something and all of a sudden you feel like everything that could go wrong does … all at the same time? This is the equivalent of "hitting the wall."

We were approaching mile 20 when Greg stopped. He said his legs felt like jelly, and he started to stretch them. We said, "Stretch as much as you need; we can walk for now." Greg was at "the wall."

He wanted to continue; he just wasn't sure how he was going to do it as his legs were unresponsive and weak. "We will finish together even if we have to walk the rest of the way," we said encouragingly. We walked mostly and jogged intermittently as Greg agonized. As we reached each mile marker, I would say "Woo hoo! Five more miles to go!" Then, "Four more; we are getting close!"

> The keys to breaking through the wall are all in the way you respond and how you've mentally prepared yourself for this moment.

Not every person has this experience of "hitting the wall." Sometimes it is not a wall but a roadblock or a bump in the road. The keys to breaking through the wall are all in the way you respond and how you've mentally prepared yourself for this moment.

As I mentioned earlier, my trainer, Chewi, had been warned about how difficult the hills were coming into Central Park towards the end of the marathon route in New York City. Besides the weather, this was another consideration and possible obstacle he was concerned about. He decided not to take any chances. The day before the marathon, he went to inspect the hills and even ran them. He thought to himself: "Not so tough."

At about mile 23 during the marathon, he was coming into Central Park and his legs started to cramp. He felt the toll of the miles he had already covered. "Whoaaaaa! Where did these hills come from? They seem a lot steeper than the ones I ran yesterday," he thought.

He was so focused on his goal that before he started the actual marathon he had decided there was no wall to face. He was prepared for all possible obstacles and, therefore, no wall showed up, rather some hills he already knew how to handle. He slowed down his pace and decided that it was more important to finish the race than to end up trying to make it under three hours and not actually making it. Secretly, he had wanted to get to the finish line before his running group. They hadn't been very encouraging about his three hour goal, and instead of being proud of how he ran with their national flag the day before the marathon, they instead pointed out what a mistake they thought he had made by doing it. He wanted to prove them wrong.

Another thing that really kept him going besides his focus and determination to finish was the other people that were running alongside him. He said many were people he would have never expected to see at such a test of endurance. People who seemed overweight, people with physical challenges (like a prosthetic leg), even people who were much older than he was. They really inspired him and motivated him to continue. If they could do it, so could he!

When I got to mile 20 in my first marathon, I knew I had already had an extraordinary experience as I was enjoying running each mile with important people in my life. As I started on this mile, I was amazed and excited about what I had already done and about how close I was to finishing. I had 10K more to go. I thought to myself "that's easy." I ran mile 20 with my best friend Nel; she is like a sister to me. We have known each other since the ninth grade. What a fun mile to reminisce on all our adventures and shared milestones in our life. Then suddenly I thought to myself, "Isn't there supposed to be some kind of wall I may run into soon?" Then, just as quickly, I said to myself, "No way. I am having too much fun to run into any walls, and besides the final five are approaching and I am determined to run with them just as I have with everyone else." I did not acknowledge the possibility of hitting this wall; I did just the opposite. It did not exist for me.

Now keep in mind, that for me, the most important thing was to finish, and I was clear that I was not in competition with the Kenyans or with anyone else for that matter. This was my personal race. It just happened that 40,000 others were also running their own race along with me. What did I do to prevent "the wall" from showing up? Mainly, I focused on enjoying my experience the way I had created it. Even though it was not necessarily how I thought it would be, it actually was much better.

Running Through Chinatown During the Chicago Marathon 2006

Imagine "What If" And Solve In Advance

How can you avoid hitting this wall? The best way to avoid or prevent the wall from showing up is to be prepared. Preparation comes from practice and repetition. I am not saying that you need to run the marathon before you actually run the marathon. I mean that in order to be ready for any challenges or obstacles that can come up on your way to your goal, you want to already anticipate them and have a strategy to overcome them if they do show up.

One thing you can do is write down your goal and brainstorm about what weaknesses or possible obstacles you can foresee that could arise on your way to achieving it. For each of these obstacles or weaknesses, identify at least three solutions or ways to overcome them. This is playing the "what if" game ... and knowing exactly how to handle any of the obstacles which could show up.

For example, suppose your goal is to lead your first workshop for a minimum of 25 people. Begin by writing down all the elements you would need to have in place in order for this to happen. You would need a venue; you would need to invite people to come to the event. Perhaps you would need to advertise. You'd also need to prepare your workshop design, practice your presentation, prepare printed materials for your participants, have a power point or keynote presentation, confirm the attendance of your guests, and so much more.

For each of these elements, write down the "what if" scenarios, and then go ahead and come up with possible solutions or ways to overcome them. As an example, let's brainstorm the "what ifs" for having a PowerPoint or keynote presentation.

What if... the light on the projector does not work?
Solutions:

- Have a spare light bulb
- Consider using a plasma or LCD to show your visual aids.
- Have the appropriate connection cables and adapters for either case.
- Be prepared to conduct your workshop without visual aids, or have a white board or easel pad as a back up.

You get the idea. Do this for each "what if" on your list.

In Chapter 2, I mentioned Charlie, Ray and Kevin, the runners who ran across the Sahara. They had many challenges and obstacles on their way to the Red Sea. Dehydration, fatigue, injuries and illness were some of the recurring challenges which the runners faced. There was one particular obstacle that became the runner's wall in this expedition. It was the uncertainty about whether or not they would be allowed to run through Lybia on their way to the Red Sea. Lybia was the safest country for them to run through; the other options were Chad and Sudan areas that had land mines and unfriendly atmospheres; in other words, these were extremely dangerous options. The director of their expedition diligently contacted the Lybian government, the United Nations, as well as all his contacts to make this happen for the runners, and it required a lot of persistence and creativity.

They had run the equivalent of 84 marathons, over 2,000 miles in nearly two months. It was becoming very difficult to continue with their run with the possibility of getting to the Lybian border and having to call it the end of their expedition. The end of their goal.

When this situation came up, Kevin, who was from Taiwan, really faced a difficult decision. He felt that the possibility of running through any other country besides Lybia was not a risk he was willing to take. He talked with his teammates and let them know he was going to go home and not finish. Charlie and Ray encouraged him, told him they knew he could do it, and told him not to quit because they were a team and wanted to finish together as a team. They convinced him to continue to run until they reached the Lybian border.

On day 65 of their expedition, they got word from the Lybian government that they could come into the country and run through it on their way to the Red Sea. They arrived at the Lybian border on day 74 after running the equivalent of 108 marathons. It took them another 25 days to run across Lybia and arrive in Egypt.

Natalie's Race

So how did Natalie prepare to break through the wall? She confessed there were a few times when she missed training runs and that fear started to set in telling her that she would not be able to complete the marathon. She told fear to take a backseat because she was the one driving this train. The other factor that really prepared her was an 80 year old man who trained with her group although at a faster pace. This man had completed 27 marathons. Whenever she thought of him, she was inspired by his commitment and passion. She would say to herself "if he can do it at his age, I have

ZERO reasons to sit on the couch making excuses." She also used the power of visualization, imagining herself running the race and completing it under her goal time of four hours, elated, full of pride and joy. The week before the race, she added her friend Lizzie to her visualization, running with her and finishing together. She was ready and very excited!

There they were at the starting line with thousands and thousands of others. It was dark and cool and about 4:30 a.m. The race was set to start at 5:00 a.m. Natalie was feeling very excited and a little nervous at the same time. She was so thrilled to be able to share this experience with her friend Lizzie which had been an unexpected addition to the already incredible experience she was about to have. "I could feel the air, thick with excitement and happiness; there were so many groups of people running for charity and doing something we could all check off our bucket list." she recalled.

The gun went off, and they started running. She shared with me that one of the coolest things was to see all the people cheering them along the route. She saw people cheering for those they knew and also cheering for the ones they didn't know just because they were running. She thought, "Wow! What a gift; these are total strangers supporting us, not expecting anything back." They got to the seventh mile marker and thought, "Wow! We still have 20 more miles to go." They would laugh and do reframing and humor to lighten the situation and their feelings. She recalls it was mostly their minds going "like are you serious?" Everything was great until mile 12 where they were both really tired, the roar of the supporters cheering them on kept them going. She was so grateful to have Lizzie battling together with her.

Disaster struck at mile 17 when Lizzie blew her knee out. Natalie felt sad for Lizzie and her injury. Lizzie told her to go on without her, otherwise she would not make her time goal. Natalie would not have it! She told Lizzie that she was more important than any completion time and that she would not go on without her. Natalie began to focus on Lizzie and how she could help her finish alongside her. At this point Natalie said to me, "the race became all about the other person versus my own personal goal." Lizzie regained her composure, and they walked and limped most of the way. It turns out that Lizzie knew she had a problem with her knee before going into the race and had decided she wanted to run it regardless. When she told Natalie this as they walked and limped, it inspired Natalie so much; she was determined to stick it out with her.

Natalie and Lizzie Running in the Hawaii Marathon 2001

"As she dragged her leg over the finish line, tears streaming down our faces, I remembered the feelings I had visualized with the Chariots of Fire theme playing in the background. We finished in over five hours; I am not sure how long it took, and I really didn't care. What mattered was that we finished." They both inspired each other!

Jeff's Story

In January 2013, while in Miami to run the half marathon, my husband and I met a wonderful runner who also sells running skirts. Her name is Michelle. We really enjoyed meeting her and hearing the story of her husband Jeff's first marathon. It really is a great example of digging deep and how we all have our own race and experiences to live. We choose how we respond and how these experiences will impact us.

Have Your Support Team In Place

Michelle agreed to train her husband for his first marathon. This was not going to be just any marathon, rather a spring marathon, which meant that the 16 weeks of training had to happen during the worst four months of weather which New York could dish out. They had no choice but to do all of their runs outside … along with lake effect snow, sleet, and downpours. She just kept telling him they were preparing for any kind of weather on race day and that "nobody ever felt better by not running." They just put their heads down and went.

This took a giant toll on their souls … and their soles. Their sneakers had become old friends by this time and were either on their feet or in their trunk. They were perfectly broken in, as Michelle put it, and they were also perfectly flat. Two weeks before the race, she bought new running shoes for herself and her husband. Same model, size, color. Same everything.

There they were the night before the marathon: clothes laid out, race bibs on shirts, race nutrition on top of outfit, sneakers with timing chips on, post race clothes ready to go and the cooler loaded with celebratory drinks, water, and food. They had their car gassed up, had double-checked their directions and had the parking figured out. They were ready. It was perfect!

They were off! As we have established, 26.2 miles is a long way no matter how you cover it. They were running at a good pace through the first part of the route. At about mile 10 of the Buffalo Marathon, Jeff looked at Michelle and said, "Man, my feet hurt." She told him "You're fine. I wonder where your parents are meeting us on the course?" They kept going.

At around mile 15 he looked at her again and said, "My feet feel like they are on fire!" She told him again that he was fine and setting such a great example for the kids. They kept going.

At mile 20, Jeff looked at Michelle with pain in his face and said, "My feet REALLY hurt." Once more, she told him, "You're fine. It's going to feel so great when people ask you what you did this weekend and you can say you ran a marathon." And once more, they kept going.

At mile 23 Michelle recalls literally smelling smoke. Thankfully Jeff's feet weren't really on fire! She said, "We only have about 5k to go." He looked at her with eyes red from salty sweat and said, "My feet are burning up!" Jeff was at the wall! Michelle again encouraged him to press on by telling him how proud she was of him. And they did just that.

They crossed the finish line upright and smiling. He did it! Jeff had accomplished one of his major life goals. He was just beaming, and Michelle couldn't have been more proud. As they walked to their car to meet friends, change clothes, and get some water, that's when he said something which shocked her.

In a painful whisper of a voice Jeff said, "I wore the wrong sneakers." Michelle struggled to understand. After a minute she realized what he meant. He had actually worn the WRONG sneakers! He had put on his "old friends" by mistake in a last minute decision before they headed out the door that morning. His old friends did not have the race chip on them, and therefore, he did not get an official time. Jeff did not officially finish his first marathon. Or did he?

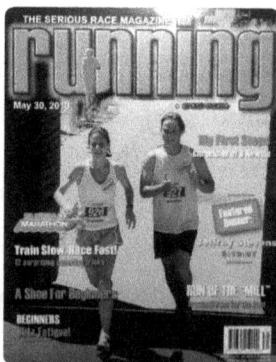

Jeff Stevens Crossing the Finish Line at the Buffalo Marathon

As I learned from Michelle, a runner's physical strength can only be surpassed by the amount of heart he or she has. No matter what anyone says, your heart knows better. The clock, the timing chip, the official results, even the phone call from your confused older brother who wants to know why you didn't finish the marathon even though he saw that your wife did. Your heart knows ...and it keeps going.

> No matter what anyone says, your heart knows better.

See Yourself At The Finish Line!

Believe it or not, this chapter has taken me the longest to write out of all the chapters in this book. What I find interesting is that it is precisely as it should be. This marks the point in my book writing where I am very close to finishing. It's a chapter where I could have very easily "hit the wall." While, I have slowed down my pace in my writing, I have never stopped. As I did during my first marathon, I have seen myself at the finish line with regards to this book and the impact it will have on your life as you are reading the words within it. It is what inspires me to keep moving forward no matter what the pace. Seeing yourself and feeling the emotions of having accomplished your goal is crucial when you are so close to getting there and are feeling like you are at "the wall" or stuck. As I was sharing this with my good friend and writing coach, Jan, she shared with me a time when she experienced hitting "the wall."

Keep Going; You Are Almost There!

She was participating in a 39 mile walk for breast cancer. When she was about six miles from the finish line, her knee really started to hurt and she began to feel like she had to stop. She had hit "the wall." She called her coach and also husband Ian and said, "We're done; it's over. My right knee is bending and not responding. Come by and pick me up in the car." He said, "You don't mean that. Come on, Jan. All you have to do is catch up to those women and ride their coat tails." Jan said, "I can't catch up with those ladies; I don't even see them. My knee is speaking to me." Then she said to him, "I'll tell you what I am going to do. I am going to go into the next aid station and get my knee wrapped, and we will see how it goes."

*Jan (far right) With Her Husband Ian (to her left) and
Fellow Participants During Her 39 Mile Breast Cancer Walk*

She arrived at the aid station, and there was a woman there helping out who happened to be a nurse and had just quit the walk herself. Jan explained her knee trouble to the woman and was told to stop the walk. Jan politely asked her to wrap it up so she could finish. The woman reluctantly did as Jan asked, stunned by her decision to continue.

Jan kept on walking and crossed the finish line exhilarated and proud. She was so happy about completing her race! Ian met her, smiling, telling her how proud he was that she had done it. He said, "I knew you could do it. I knew you wanted to finish. I knew that all you needed was some encouragement."

The only way you won't make it is if you quit!

The importance of having the right people on your team and being prepared for when unimaginable things happen is crucial to your success. As long as you keep going, even if at a slower pace, unsure of the route you are going to take, with a wrapped knee, or even burning feet. The only way you won't make it is if you quit! Keep going. You are almost there! You can do it!

Chapter 8 Action Steps

"It does not matter how slowly you go as long as you do not stop."

Confucius

1. Write all important elements necessary for accomplishing your goal, and write out every "what if" you can think of, and come up with at least three solutions for each "what if."
2. Have your support team in place and prepare them to encourage you, especially when you say you want to stop or quit when you think you can't go on. They know better!
3. See yourself at the finish line and feel the emotions of having accomplished your goal. This will give you extra energy and motivation!
4. Keep going; you are almost there!

Chapter 9

You Did It!!!

“ *What you get by achieving your goals is not as important as what you become by achieving your goals.”*

Henry David Thoreau

Remember Greg? Well, after walking and jogging intermittently for most of the miles after mile 15, we came upon the 25th mile marker. I said, "Okay Greg, once we get to that mile marker, we will be a little over a mile from the finish line. What do you say if we run it?" Greg just nodded. We crossed it, and he darted in front of us, running as Antonio and I looked at each other in amazement. He was going for it. He could taste victory!

It was so exciting to watch him and to run with him in what ended up being his fastest mile of the whole marathon. Greg fought back the tears from the overwhelming emotion as he made it across the finish line. We crossed it together! We did it! "Greg, you did it!" He was in so much pain, yet he was so happy. He couldn't believe he had done it. He felt incredible and was so thankful that he did not give up, that we believed in him, and encouraged him the whole way.

Greg, Me and Antonio Crossing the Finish Line Together in Chicago 2009

Happy With Our Finisher Medals Chicago 2009

For Greg, finishing the Chicago Marathon showed him he could do anything he set his mind to, especially when so many people had said he couldn't do it. Now when he finds himself in situations where others are thinking and saying that there is no way they can do a certain thing, Greg says "We've got this. We can do it!" And together, they always end up succeeding.

When Charlie, Ray and Kevin finally made it to the Red Sea after 111 days of non-stop running through 140 degree temperatures, injuries, sandstorms, dehydration, navigation problems, and the uncertainty of continuing their journey through Lybia, there were many emotions and feelings that they all experienced. Despite the difficulties encountered during the expedition, as well as the many trials and tribulations which they overcame, they never took a day off. And when they saw and touched the Red Sea, it was all worth it!

Ray learned from running the Sahara "that any limitations that we have are limitations that we have set upon ourselves. If you think you can only run 5K, then you will only run that far. It's where you set those goals because, really, there are no boundaries. I am living proof of that."

> "It's where you set those goals because really, there are no boundaries..."

Ray and his friends had originally set out on an 80 day expedition across the Sahara Desert and wound up traveling much further. They became a lot more than just three runners with a big goal. They became inspired by the people they met on their journey and founded www.H2OAfrica.org, an organization to raise money and create awareness for clean, safe water in Africa.

Approaching My First Marathon Finish Line

I had just finished the final five, during which I ran with the future in-laws whom I was just starting to know, my beloved dog Nina, my jogging club 1427, my soon-to-be-born niece Irene Sofia, my past love, and finally, my future husband, Antonio.

Enjoy Your Success!

It is hard to describe the feelings and emotions I felt when I was approaching the finish line. I was overwhelmed by the pride and the feeling of accomplishment; I felt pain, love, relief, excitement, and euphoria, as I relished every single experience!

Me Crossing the Finish Line of My First Marathon 2006

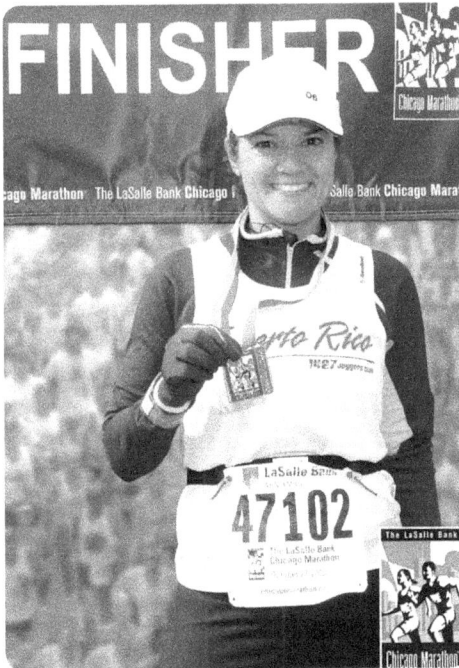

Incredibly Proud to Have Completed my First Marathon in Chicago 2006

My good friend, Kellie, met me at the finish line with a bouquet of flowers. In Chicago, they do a great job of making the marathon finishers feel proud and special. In many places, if you wear your medal after the event, there are special offers or even giveaways. Everyone on the street congratulates the marathoners as they celebrate with each other. Kellie and I enjoyed a free bottle of wine, because I was wearing my medal, while we enjoyed a great steak at Smith & Wollensky as we commemorated my victory!

Celebrating After my First Marathon with my friend Kellie at Smith and Wollensky

Make Sure You Celebrate!

Celebrating your accomplishment is a huge part of accomplishing your goal, so make sure you have planned for it or are prepared to celebrate even if all the details of it are not clear. Just giving yourself that space for recognition and reward, be it of your own making or be it from others, is essential to the completion of the experience of attaining your goal.

Some ideas of celebrations or rewards you can look forward to are:

- Having a party.
- Planning a special dinner at your favorite restaurant.
- Taking a reward vacation to a place you have always wanted to visit.
- Giving to a cause that you really believe in.
- Buying yourself something that you have always wanted but couldn't justify.

By now you should have come up with many ideas that speak to you and the things that you most enjoy and treasure.

My Finish Line

When I finished my first marathon, one of the first thoughts that came to me which I shared with Kellie was that everyone should run a marathon even if just once. That was how powerful the experience was for me. It was not so much about running the 26.2 miles, rather it was about who I had become in the process. That was my biggest reward and no one could take it away from me. After accomplishing this, I felt there was nothing I couldn't do.

It was not so much about running the 26.2 miles, rather it was about who I had become in the process.

I ran my next marathon in historic Berlin, Germany. Our running club was participating in this marathon as a group. There were several club members for whom this would be their first marathon. I especially remember Doña Ana as we affectionately call her. Doña Ana was 68 years old when she ran the Berlin marathon. I was so impressed with her, especially when I learned her age and heard she had only been running for about three years.

Doña Ana's First Marathon

I asked what motivated her to run a marathon and she shared her story. Her doctor had insisted that she start to walk in order to improve her arthritis condition. So she started walking. Her daughter is also a member of our running club, and she suggested Ana become part of it since walkers could also participate. Chewi, our trainer and coach, gave her training tables to follow. She began to see amazing improvements in her ability to walk and in the reduction of symptoms from her arthritis. She began to jog as well as walk, and pretty soon she felt very comfortable jogging and decided to run a 10K race. She finished in 1:35:00, as she recalls with great enthusiasm.

Chewi encouraged her to participate and run the Berlin Marathon, which would take place just shy of two years after she had run her first 10K. At first when she heard how long the marathon was, she would say to herself, "No. That you cannot do." Chewi thought differently, so she trusted him and registered for the marathon not knowing how she was going to do it, yet knowing that he had helped many others do it before her.

Just as before, he gave her training tables in order to prepare, and she followed them to the letter. She told me she remembers every detail about this marathon. "It was my first; you always remember everything about the first."

On September 30, 2007, the day of her first marathon, she didn't know what she didn't know; she just kept running. She did not pay attention to the time or the pace; she was in the moment! She was enjoying the scenery and historical significance of the route. There was live music and people everywhere; it was beautiful! She recounted this to me and said, "Once I realized I was at the 30 kilometer mark, I knew I was going to finish."

I asked her what it was like for her when she saw the finish line coming into view. "My first reaction," she said, "was to cry from happiness and my accomplishment. I ran the whole time and didn't walk a step." She finished in 5:04:42. She even surprised our trainer, who expected her to cross the finish line at about 5:30:00. "I felt so good," she told me, "that I even wore heels to our celebration dinner that night. This was not only my first marathon; it was also the first time I had a beer!"

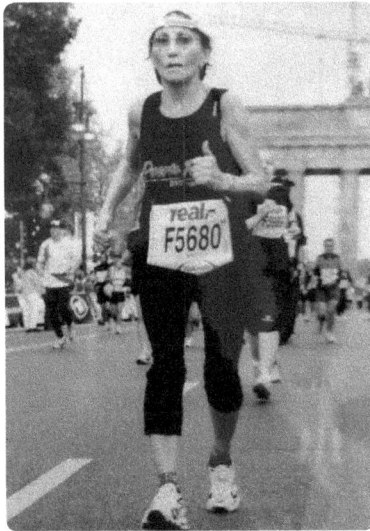

Doña Ana Running the Berlin Marathon

Doña Ana says that achieving this goal gave her the confidence that she could do it again, and she has completed various marathons since then. In 2010, she ran the Athens Marathon in Greece and won 3rd place in her age category with a finish time of 5:12:00. She was also 70 years old by then! She was set to run in the New York City Marathon in 2012 except that it got cancelled due to the passing of hurricane Sandy, which affected the area days before the marathon was scheduled to occur. In 2013 she was able to run the New York City Marathon, completing it in 6:01:06, at 73 years old! Since then she has participated in many other races. Go Ana, Go!

Doña Ana Crossing the Finish Line of Her First Marathon in Berlin 2007

Celebrating Completing the Berlin Marathon with Doña Ana in 2007

Chewi's Finish Line

Chewi did get to the finish line in New York City with a time of 3:02:00. And yes... he was the first among his running club participants to finish. His brother, Manuel, met him at the finish line full of emotion and very proud. He is also a runner, so he knew what it meant to accomplish such an important and significant goal.

Chewi Running in Puerto Rico

As a result of finishing his first marathon and having the experience he did during the event, Chewi came back home with a new awareness and a new purpose. He realized that anything can be achieved if you set your mind to it. He also learned that you have to go through the experience yourself in order to not only understand it but to undergo the growth that comes from taking the actions, overcoming obstacles, and staying your course on your way to your goal.

As long as you take the steps and actions necessary to achieve your goal, you will succeed. Chewi wanted to challenge the myth that only elite runners could run marathons, and by achieving it himself, he was inspired to help others do the same. He now knew that the only limitations people really have are the ones they impose upon themselves. He had witnessed people of all ages, fitness levels, weights, and even disabilities participating in the marathon. Not just participating...finishing!

> If you have the right mentality and expectations, you can achieve anything you set your sights on.

He also learned that achieving any goal was a lot more mental than anything else, that if you have the right mentality and expectations, you can achieve anything you set your sights on.

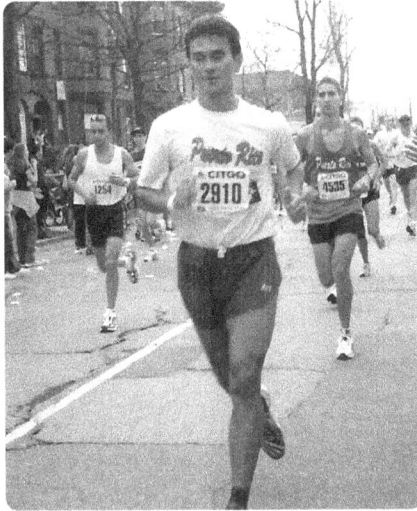

Chewi Running in the Boston Marathon in 2002

Ask What's Next

For Chewi, running his first marathon was the beginning of a way of life, a way of taking on big challenges which others would find too difficult to attempt. Since then, he has trained and taken countless groups of novice and experienced runners to marathons all over the world. He founded a running club, has become involved in projects on the island which help people become healthier and more physically fit. He has also opened two athletic stores which he operates with his wife, Maria. And for himself, he has completed 3 Iron Man Competitions and continues to challenge himself and others to be their best physically and mentally.

Chewi During the Louiseville Ironman in 2012

*Chewi Showing Off His Ironman Finisher Medal in
Louiseville, Kentucky in 2012*

His most cherished project is the one called "Patitas Calientes" which means "hot legs" in Spanish. He has 21 groups of people who are 60 years old and older whom he trains daily in different towns on the island. He does this to help them maintain good physical and mental condition, as well as to contribute to their social life with different activities. This population, he believes, suffers a lot from being forgotten and neglected, especially by their adult children. This effort has had a huge impact on the quality of life for this generation and has helped them continue to be an active group of people in our community.

Chewi Exercising With His "Patitas Calientes" in Puerto Rico

For Natalie, the experience of running and completing her first marathon with her friend Lizzie strengthened their friendship and reminded her that life is always about the journey rather than the endpoint. In her words, "after running my first marathon, I knew that I could accomplish anything; all I had to do was set my intention, be clear about my action steps, complete them, and smile lots during the process. Whenever I get nervous or fearful, I remember that persistence is the key to all successful endeavors. I just have to keep putting one foot in front of the other and before I know it, I'll be running through the finish line feeling the breeze of sweet success on my face. Victory!"

Natalie has checked off many other things from her bucket list since her experience in Honolulu in December of 2001. The belief and certainty she gained from her experience helped her be able to climb a mountain and then jump off a waterfall in Costa Rica. She claims that the marathon experience really gives you the confidence to do anything because your mind is the one in charge of your physical experience.

Did wearing the wrong sneakers and not having his first marathon officially timed and in the books make that event irrelevant for

Jeff? Absolutely not. Even though Jeff's name does not appear on the official finisher list of the Buffalo Marathon, nor can he, or anyone else for that matter, look up his official time for the event, none of these things matter. Those are external symbols of accomplishment, and they are for the people that are not that important.

We carry our symbols of accomplishment within ourselves and in our heart. Jeff experienced and ran his first marathon and he knows it from the deepest corner of his soul, as does his wife Michelle. She not only witnessed his heroic resolve to finish, she was his ROCK, his biggest fan, his biggest cheerleader and believer in his ability to do it! And for her he is forever grateful, even when his feet were burning up...and he didn't quite feel that way!

> We carry our symbols of accomplishment within ourselves and in our heart.

Because he completed the Buffalo Marathon, Jeff gained the confidence and faith to move across the country and start his own company! With a heart and soul like Jeff's, success is in his footsteps. Keep on running!

Keep Running Your Race

One of the messages and insights I want you to take away from this book and the stories within it is that we all have our own race to create and experience. Even if we share a common goal, our journey along the way will not be the same; rather, it will be unique to each of us and that is what makes it so significant and special.

> We all have our own race to create and experience.

Chapter 9 Action Steps

"To finish first, you must finish."

Rick Mears

1. Enjoy your success!
2. Make sure you celebrate; this is a big deal! You have worked hard and you deserve the reward!
3. Ask what's next. You have the confidence and the experience now!
4. Keep running your race; it is ever-changing and exciting!

Chapter 10

Let's Go!

"*Go for it now. The future is promised to no one.***"**

Wayne Dyer

W e have been on a journey from deciding what we want, to creating a plan, taking action, and accomplishing what we set out to do. Now it's your turn to implement your plan ... and just go!

I love the lyrics from a recent Calvin Harris song called very appropriately "Let's Go." It truly has become an anthem for me when I am in the groove, inspired, and moving towards my goals, and also when I'm not feeling so inspired. It really gets my juices flowing and prompts me to just go!

Lyrics:

> *Let's go!*
> *Make no excuses now*
> *I'm talking here and now*
> *I'm talking here and now*
> *Let's go!*
> *Your time is running out*
> *I'm talking here and now*
> *I'm talking here and now*
>
> *It's not about what you've done*
> *It's about what you're doing*
> *It's all about where you're going*
> *No matter where you've been*
> *Let's go!...*

> It's not about
> what you've done
> It's about what
> you're doing
> It's all about where
> you're going
> No matter where
> you've been
> Lets go!...

Now it's your turn to take the action steps and start running your race, no matter what you intend to achieve.

Let's review the process. To make it easier, at the end of this book you will find a list of all the action steps mentioned in each chapter. Review this list to remind yourself of some helpful activities and actions.

First, unearth the dreams that might be buried under programming from parents, teachers, peers, etc. The activities in chapter one can assist you. Next, take 100% responsibility for your life and wellbeing. Remember, you create your outcomes by changing and being aware of your responses. The thoughts you think, the actions you take, and the images you focus on...these are all within your control.

Begin by choosing one goal to focus on. Develop precise clarity around this goal; be specific with it. How much? By when? Find a mentor or coach to help you. Share your goal with your inner circle, (spouse, close friends, children) and explain what is involved and why you want to achieve it. It's important to tell them what's in it for them as well.

Take the first step! Divide the overall goal into manageable actions. Practice 5 and goal and pay attention to feedback and adjust as needed.

Assemble your team! Visualize yourself achieving your goal and how you will feel when you do it! Show up on race day, pace yourself, enjoy the journey, expect to finish, expect to succeed!

> Show up on race day, pace yourself, enjoy the journey, expect to fin-ish, expect to succeed!

Celebrate your milestones on the way to your goal. Rely on your team for encouragement and support. Keep taking action even if you slow your pace; this will ensure you are keeping the momentum. Anticipate the "what ifs" and have your team ready to encourage you, especially when you say you want to quit.

See yourself at the finish line and feel the emotions of having accomplished your goal! Keep going! You are so close!

Celebrate! You deserve it!

What will you do NOW? I want to know, so please share your stories of achievement and success with me at www.run-your-race.com.

Finishing my first marathon had a huge impact on me, as I have shared in the pages of this book. In particular, I want to mention the incredible confidence and courage I have gained as a result of going for the things that I really want to experience in this life without holding back. Since then, I have completed two other full marathons, countless half-marathons, married the man of my dreams, started a coaching and training business, spoken to many groups about principles of success and how to achieve and live the life of their dreams, and finally I have written my first book. A book which I hope has inspired, motivated, and above all encouraged you to take action towards living on your terms, striving for your dreams, and running YOUR RACE!

> Live on your terms, strive for your dreams and keep running your race!

Run Your Race
Action Steps

Chapter 1 Action Steps

"Twenty years from now you will be more disappointed by the things you didn't do than by the ones you did do. So throw off the bowlines, sail away from the safe harbor. Catch the trade winds in your sails. Explore. Dream. Discover."

Mark Twain

1. Answer the question: What would you do if you could not fail?
2. Take your power back and exercise your right to choose when given the opportunity.
3. Ask a trusted loved one or friend to challenge you for five minutes by repeatedly asking "What do you want?" and write down all your answers.
4. Make a list of 101 goals.
5. Take 100% responsibility. You can create the outcome you want by changing your response.
6. Stop imagining negative outcomes and eliminate your fear.
7. Create a Victory log of your wins and daily successes.

Chapter 2 Action Steps

"You can have anything you want, if you want it badly enough. You can be anything you want to be, do anything you set out to accomplish if you hold to that desire with singleness of purpose."

Abraham Lincoln

1. Choose one goal to focus on.
2. Be very clear on the goal and put a time frame on it. (How much, by when?)
3. Find a mentor or coach (through books, online, or in your community)
4. Do research on your goal. (What skills are needed to accomplish your goal?)
5. Review your Victory Log often.
6. Write your reasons for wanting to accomplish your goal. (Display them where you can see them daily.)
7. Share your goal with your inner circle. (spouse, children, close friends)

Chapter 3 Action Steps

"A journey of a thousand miles must begin with a single step."

Lao Tzu

1. Take the first step.
2. Divide into manageable actions.
3. Practice 5 and Goal.
4. Pay attention to feedback and adjust when needed.
5. Continue to take steps.

Chapter 4 Action Steps

"There is no such thing as a self made man. You will reach your goals only with the help of others."

George Shinn

1. Find a mentor or coach (if you don't have one already).
2. Share your vision and goal with your inner circle (spouse, children, close friends) and explain to them what is involved in your achieving this goal.
3. Get an accountability partner.
4. Form or join a Master Mind Group.
5. Identify others wanting to achieve your same goal or something similar.
6. Identify your rocks.
7. Share your vision to identify your cheerleaders.
8. Identify your possibility channels and your dead ends.
9. Go to the "Bellagio" when you encounter energy suckers.

Chapter 5 Action Steps

"Whatever the mind can conceive and believe it can achieve."

Napoleon Hill

1. Practice visualizing (start with something familiar).
2. Write out your ideal scene with every detail and incorporate all senses and feelings (remember to be very specific).
3. Create a Vision Board or Goals Book.
4. Visualize daily (see yourself in the present moment achieving your goal).

Chapter 6 Action Steps

"It is only the first step that is difficult."

Marie De Vichy-Chamrond

1. Show Up!
2. Pace yourself!
3. If you have a false start, start again!
4. Enjoy the journey; expect to finish; expect to succeed!

Chapter 7 Action Steps

"It was character that got us out of bed, commitment that moved us into action, and discipline that enabled us to follow through."

Zig Ziglar

1. Celebrate your accomplishments; acknowledge that you are halfway there!
2. Rely on your team for encouragement and support to keep your momentum going.
3. Keep taking steps, even if you must slow your pace.

Chapter 8 Action Steps

"It does not matter how slowly you go as long as you do not stop."

Confucius

1. Write all important elements necessary for accomplishing your goal, and write out every "what if" you can think of, and come up with at least three solutions for each "what if."
2. Have your support team in place and prepare them to encourage you, especially when you say you want to stop or quit when you think you can't go on. They know better!
3. See yourself at the finish line and feel the emotions of having accomplished your goal. This will give you extra energy and motivation!
4. Keep going; you are almost there!

Chapter 9 Action Steps

"To finish first, you must finish."

Rick Mears

1. Enjoy your success!
2. Make sure you celebrate; this is a big deal! You have worked hard and you deserve the reward!
3. Ask what's next. You have the confidence and the experience now!
4. Keep running your race; it is ever-changing and exciting!

Run Your Race—Resources

Run Your Race—online—This is an online course that takes you deeper into the concepts and actions steps laid out in this guide, with examples and tools to accomplish your goals faster. www.mayrallado.com.

Run Your Race—The Experience—This is a live experiential training with online group coaching sessions of the Run Your Race framework. To learn more, go to www.mayrallado.com.

Coaching— To accomplish goals that seem imposible as you have read it's important to have the appropriate support team. A coach is an essential part of your success team. Dr. Mayra Llado offers group and individual coaching programs. For more information on her coaching you can go to: www.mayrallado.com.

EFT (Emotional Freedom Technique)—Developed originally by Roger Callahan then improved upon by Gary Craig who named it EFT. It is an emotional version of acupuncture, except there are no needles involved. It incorporated mentally, tuning into certain issues while tapping on certain meridian points with your fingertips. Properly done, EFT appears to balance disturbances in the meridian system. For more information, go to www.runyourracebook.com.

The Sedona Method—Originally created by Lester Levenson and now taught and shared worldwide by one of his students Hale Dwoskin. It is a simple way you can learn how to tap into your natural ability to let go of any unwanted or painful feeling. Through a series of questions, you go through the experience of welcoming and becoming aware of what you are feeling and gently guide yourself into letting go. To learn more about the Sedona Method, go to www.sedona.com.

RIM (Regenerating Images in Memory)—Created and developed by Dr. Deb Sandella. In her words, "RIM initially began as a synthesis of techniques that access the subconscious mind directly-Somatic Therapy, Ericksonian Hypnosis and Interactive Guided Imagery and has continued to expand and evolve. Originally, the acronym RIM stood for my book Releasing the Inner Magician so it could be conveniently referenced as a research intervention for people suffering with IBS (Irritable Bowel Syndrome). This study found that RIM significantly decreases the symptoms of stress-related illness and significantly increases one's quality of life (Boxwell Dissertation, Holos University, 2004). As it has evolved into a scientific method, the meaning of RIM has become both: Re-generating Images in Memory and Re-creating the Inner Movie. You get the idea!" To find a RIM facilitator or learn more about the process, go to www.riminstitute.com.

5 and Goal Sample Checklist—to download a template to use this action item checklist on a daily basis, go to www.runyourrace-book.com.

Master Mind Group Format—to download a sample of a format to follow to conduct a Master Mind Meeting, go to www.runyourrace-book.com.

Visualization Resources—view a tutorial on creating an audio recording with images for your use as a visualization tool; go to www.runyourracebook.com.

A great book to get you started with visualization and having a lot of fun in the process is: *Fun With Visualization* by Starr Pilmore.

Vision Board Examples—to view examples of Vision Boards, go to www.runyourracebook.com.

What If? Worksheet—to download and print a What If? Worksheet, go to www.runyourracebook.com.

Run Your Race—References

Byrne, Rhonda. The Secret. New York: Atria Books, 2006.

Canfield, Jack and Janet Switzer. The Success Principles: How to Get from Where You Are to Where You Want to Be. New York: Harper Collins Publisher, 2005.

Harris, Calvin. Let's Go: Song. Columbia. Deconstruction. Fly Eye. Ultra. 2012.

Hill, Napoleon. Think and Grow Rich. California: Highroads Media, Inc., 2008.

Nall, Sam. It's Only a Mountain: Dick and Rick Hoyt, Men of Iron. Florida: Charybdis Publishing, 2002.

Pascual-Leon, Alvaro. The Brain That Plays Music and Is Changed by It. (2001) Behavioral Neurology Unit, Beth Israel Deaconess Medical Center, Harvard Medical School, Boston, Massachusetts 02215, USA.

Running The Sahara: Documentary. Dir. James Moll. DVD. NEHST, 2007.

Star Wars: Episode V—The Empire Strikes Back. Movie. Dir. Irvin Kershner. Lucasfilm, 1980.

Wattles, Wallace D. The Science of Getting Rich: Harnessing the Power of Creative Thought. Holyoke, Mass : E. Towne, 1910.

About the Author

Dr. Mayra Lladó is an architect of the smile and of life. She is the owner of San Juan Smile Spa in San Juan, Puerto Rico where she provides Cosmetic Dentistry services in a spa environment.

In addition to helping people have beautiful smiles, her passion is helping people discover their purpose and unwrap their gifts. Dr. Mayra has studied and applied principles of success since the year 2000 and has helped thousands of business owners, with varied experience and backgrounds, create more success in their business and in their lives through the services she and her husband Antonio provide through their company Success In Action.

She is the author of the best selling book: *Run Your Race: a Guide to Making Your Impossibles Possible*, Co-Author of the best selling book: *Success University For Women*, Co-Author of the book *Live Your Passion*, International Speaker, Trainer and High Performance Coach.

She has been personally mentored by Jack Canfield, author of The Success Principles and contributor in The Secret, is a graduate of his Train the Trainer program and has had the honor and privilege to serve on the assisting team of many of his live events including Breakthrough to Success and Train the Trainer.

Dr. Mayra has given speeches to business owners, the general public, women recovering from addictions, and high school students among other groups.

She is the founder and CEO of Success In Action Inc., a company that provides High Performance Coaching and Experiential workshops and trainings to individuals and businesses.

Her trainings and retreats focus on Maximizing your potential, Igniting Your Success and Running Your Race. They are for entrepreneurs, sales people, educators, industry leaders, consultants and you who does not settle and wants to be the best version of yourself. Take advantage of your talents to experience the life you have the power to create; one of passion, fulfillment, joy and success.

To find out more about Dr. Mayra's workshops and trainings, books, audios, and other materials, or to inquire about her availability as a speaker, coach or trainer, you can contact her office at:

Success In Action Inc.
P.O. Box 193805
San Juan, PR 00919-3805
info@mayrallado.com

To reclaim your power and live with passion go to:

www.mayrallado.com
www.runyourracebook.com